Property and Trust Law in the Czech Republic

Property and Trust Law in the Czech Republic

Kateřina Ronovská
Eva Dobrovolná
Bohumil Havel
Vlastimil Pihera

This book was originally published as a monograph in the International Encyclopaedia of Laws/Property and Trust Law.

Founding Editor: Roger Blanpain, Frank Hendrickx
General Editor: Alain Verbeke
Volume Editors: Alain Verbeke & Vincent Sagaert

Wolters Kluwer

Published by:
Kluwer Law International B.V.
PO Box 316
2400 AH Alphen aan den Rijn
The Netherlands
E-mail: international-sales@wolterskluwer.com
Website: lrus.wolterskluwer.com

Sold and distributed by:
Wolters Kluwer Legal & Regulatory U.S.
7201 McKinney Circle
Frederick, MD 21704
United States of America
Email: customer.service@wolterskluwer.com

ISBN 978-94-035-2733-8

e-Book: ISBN 978-94-035-2734-5
web-PDF: ISBN 978-94-035-2735-2

This title is available on www.kluwerlawonline.com

The Authors

Kateřina Ronovská is as an associate professor, a Head of the Department of Civil Law at the Faculty of Law, Masaryk University, Brno. She teaches Civil law, Foundation and Trust law and is involved in the systematic study of this field in the European context. She is the author of numerous publications (books and commentaries) and articles in professional journals. She is actively involved in international projects of comparative law. She is a member of the Scientific Board of Faculty of Law at Masaryk University and the Finance and Legislative Committee of the Government Council for non-governmental organisations.

Bohumil Havel graduated from the Faculty of Law in Pilsen, Czech Republic, works as scientific researcher in the Institute of Law of the Czech Academy of Science and teaches insolvency law in the Faculty of Law at Charles University in Prague. Objects of his scientific interest are civil law – an area of legal persons, corporate and insolvency law. He was co-drafter of the Czech Insolvency Act and the main drafter of the Czech Companies Act. He is a member of various committees, e.g., Legislative Council of the Czech government, the committee for insolvency law in Ministry of Justice. He published several books and many of articles in professional journals, including participation in the leading commentary to Companies Act. He also works as a counsel in a big Czech law firm.

The Authors

Vlastimil Pihera graduated from the Faculty of Law in Pilsen, Czech Republic, works as a scientific researcher in the Institute of Law of the Czech Academy of Science and as the Partner of Kocián Šolc Balaštík law firm in Prague. Vlastimil focuses on corporate law and the law of financial markets. He has published several books and articles in professional journals, including participation in a leading commentary to Act on Banks.

Eva Dobrovolná is Assistant Professor at the Department of Civil Procedure Law, Faculty of Law, Masaryk University, Brno. She teaches and publishes in property law and civil procedure law. She is also of counsel in an international law firm seated in Vienna. Eva is a member of expert group on new Czech Civil Procedure Code. She is a fellow of the International Society of Civile Procedure Law (Zivilprozessrechtslehrervereinigung) and teaches and publishes occasionally in Austria and Germany.

Table of Contents

Table of Contents

List of Abbreviations

ABC	Act on Business Corporations No. 90/2012 Coll.
ABGB	Austrian (General) Civil Code
BA	Building Act No. 183/2006 Coll.
CC	Civil Code No. 89/2012 Coll.
CC 1964	Civil Code No. 40/1964 Coll.
CCR	Constitution of the Czech Republic
CFRF	Czech Charter of Fundamental Rights and Freedoms
CPC	Civil Procedure Code No. 99/1963 Coll).
EA	Expropriation Act No. 184/2006 Sb.
EPC	Enforcement Procedure Code No. 120/2001 Coll.
IA	Insolvency Act No. 182/2006 Coll.
ICIF	Act on Investment Companies and Investment Funds No. 240/2013 Coll.
LRA	Land Register Act No. 256/2013 Coll.
SJP	Act on Special Judicial Proceedings No. 292/2013 Coll.
QCC	Civil Code of Québec

List of Abbreviations

General Introduction

§1. General Background of the Country

I. Geography

1. The Czech Republic is located in Central Europe in the moderate climate zone. It has the land area of 78,866 km^2 and is populated approximately with 10.6 million inhabitants. It borders Austria in the south, Germany in the west, Poland in the north and Slovakia in the east. Most of the territory is located in the geologically stable Czech massif, and a small part in the geologically younger Western Carpathians. The territory of the Czech Republic is characterised by chains of mountain ranges all along its borders, which make the country's outline clearly apparent also on geographic maps. The most important river is the Elbe, which empties into the North Sea near the Germany's port city of Hamburg.

II. Cultural Situation

2. While the beginnings of the Czech state date back to the ninth century, its present shape became stabilised in the middle of the eleventh century, without any major subsequent changes. From the historical and administrative points of view, it is thus one of the historically most stable state units in Europe.

3. Culturally, the Czech lands started their development in the context of the Holy Roman Empire (*Sacrum Imperium Romanum*). The Czech king was one of the most significant electors, i.e., a member of the electoral college of the Holy Roman Empire (there were seven electors until the seventeenth century). The most important Czech King was Charles IV, who has been dubbed 'the father of the country'. In 1526, when the representatives of the Czech nobility elected Ferdinand I Habsburg as the Czech king (who was also the emperor of the Holy Roman Empire), a union between the Czech lands and Austria (as well as Hungary) was established that lasted, in the form of Austrian and later Austro-Hungarian Monarchy, until 1918. The historical and cultural contacts with Austria were severed during the First World War, which resulted in the break-up of the Austro-Hungarian Monarchy and the establishment of two independent countries: the Austrian Republic and Czechoslovakia. The latter was a new state formed from the union of the Czech lands and northern Hungary.

4. Since the Middle Ages, the Czech lands had an ethnic structure typical of eastern Europe: the coexistence and mutual influence between German and Slavic people. Although the Czechoslovak Republic was established on a nationalist basis in 1918 (i.e., as a nation of 'Czechoslovaks'), the influence of Austrian (German) culture was always apparent, and it is still evident until this day – both as regards culture and law.

5. After the Second World War, Czechoslovakia became a part of the Soviet zone, which led to the establishment of a Communist dictatorship in 1948. The attempts at liberalisation in 1968 resulted in an invasion of armies of the Warsaw Pact (i.e., the Soviet Union and its vassal countries). The Communist regime collapsed in 1989 alongside similar regimes across the former Soviet bloc. The regime change occurred in a peaceful manner of what came to be called 'the velvet revolution'. The world-famous dramatist Václav Havel was elected the President of free Czechoslovakia. Shortly afterwards, however, nationalist tensions between the Czechs and the Slovaks resurfaced, culminating in the break-up of Czechoslovakia in 1992 into two independent countries: the Czech Republic, existing within the historical boundaries of the Czech lands, and Slovakia. Ever since, both countries have been essentially moving along the path determined by the 1989 changes.

III. Political System

6. The Czech Republic is a pluralist representative democracy. The executive power is delegated to the president and the government, which is headed by the prime minister. The legislative power is formed by a two-chamber parliament and the judicial power operates as a four-part judicial system. The highest units are the Supreme Court and the Supreme Administrative Court, with the Constitutional Court having a special position.

§2. Legal Background of the Country

I. Legal Family or Tradition

7. The Czech legal system belongs to continental law, being historically based on Roman law. Decisive for its development was the substantial (dominant) dependency on the Austrian legal system because the Czech lands were a part of the Habsburg Monarchy for several centuries. However, the shape of modern Czech private law has been affected by other sources of inspiration as well. This concerns, for instance, German law, which has affected law of obligations and corporate law. Soviet legal doctrine was likewise influential in the past, having affected the Czech legal system during the period of communism. Moreover, some legal regulations originating from the 1960s are still in effect (e.g., in the area of civil procedure) and, in many respects, they have retained their 'socialist spirit' despite numerous amendments.

8. Similar to other European continental law jurisdictions, the fundamental point of departure is the unity and incontestability of the legal order. Czech law is grounded in a formally legal dualism of public law and private law. However, no clear line can be drawn between private and public law and no legal regulation can set any binding criteria for distinguishing between the two. Being in a mutual interplay, they affect each other. Many private law acts also have certain public law consequences (e.g., as regard taxation).

9. Public law serves to protect public interest (i.e., the society as a whole), delimiting, above all, the rights and obligations of bodies of public power. At the very top of the legal system is the Constitution of the Czech Republic (CCR), which includes the Czech Charter of Fundamental Rights and Freedoms (CFRF). It is based on natural law, reflecting international covenants on human rights and fundamental freedoms.

10. Private law is, on a general level, understood as an instrument for the realisation of an individual person's freedom. In an objective sense of the word it is a part of the legal system whose written and unwritten rules regulate the mutual rights and obligations in private interactions.

Since a comparative historical perspective is helpful in understanding the substance of specific legal institutes, we consider it important to provide some broader context for the currently valid Czech legal regulation.

A. *Czech Lands as a Part of Austria-Hungary*

11. Historically, the development of private law in the Czech lands was, due to being part of the multinational Habsburg monarchy, substantially influenced by the legislative unification projects that culminated in the adoption of the Austrian Civil Code (ABGB), in effect in the Czech lands and Austria since 1811. Its natural law basis and the long time of its preparation meant that the code was able to accommodate, without any major changes, to the economic, social and political changes of the late nineteenth and early twentieth centuries. The Austrian legal order was characterised, among other things, by a partial duality of civil and business law.

B. *From the Establishment of Czechoslovakia until the 1948 Communist Coup*

12. After the formation of independent Czechoslovakia in 1918, the then current Austrian legal order was taken over on the basis of a so-called reception norm (ABGB was valid only in the Czech lands; by contrast, in Slovakia and Ruthenia, the partially codified Hungarian law was valid). As that situation caused many problems in the operation of the newly established state, there was intensive work on the unification of Czech and Slovak law during the inter-war period. That effort culminated in the government draft proposal of the Civil Code (CC) in 1937. However, due to the worsening situation, both international and national, it could not be adopted.

C. Communist Law

13. The communist coup in February 1948 and the subsequent events had fatal consequences for the further development of the legal system. Everything was done in the interest of the communist collectivist ideology. Law (including private law) was considered as a bourgeois relic that would not be needed in the future. In the meantime, law became an instrument of regulation and was meant to contribute to the construction of a 'socialist society'. As part of the so-called legislative two-year plan, the CC (Act No. 141/1950 Sb.) was adopted. The CC was characterised by its ideological basis, the privileging of the interests of the whole, and an overall simplification. It must be added, however, that the code still contained features of standard law because it was drafted, among others, by lawyers educated during the time of freedom.

14. The key element in the deconstruction of private law was the radical limitation of one's freedom of ownership and disposition. In addition to the dispossession of private property, (private) business activities were banned and other economic and political rights and freedoms became limited. The previously acknowledged concept of uniform ownership (i.e., the idea that ownership rights of people are subject to the same protection) became fragmented, the superficiality principle was abandoned, and the chance to dispose of one's property during life and after death became limited. After 1950, testamentary freedom was limited by the adoption of a ban on any conditions in last wills, and it became no longer possible to dispose of one's property by means of an inheritance contract or legacy or by making a gift *mortis causa*.

In addition, following the Soviet legal doctrine, the 1960s saw a fragmentation of private law into many independent (so-called complex) branches of law, which resulted in the loss of its internal cohesion. The CC, the economic code, the labour code, the family act and the international business code were adopted in short succession, essentially independent of each other.

15. The main features of the socialist CC 1964 were its strong ideological character and paternalism, the abandonment of traditional institutes (e.g., contracts) and terminology, and its focus on mere satisfaction of citizens' personal needs. Due to that, the regulation became removed not only from standard continental law regulations but also from the actual functioning of the society. Eventually, it became evident that such a model was inadequate both for business operations between state-owned organisations and for international business. For that reason, many traditional features of civil and business law reappeared, with the aim of regulating such relations, in the international business code and the economic code.

D. The Transformation Period

16. At the beginning of the 1990s, it was necessary to modify the Czech legal system to accommodate to the new situation arising from the major social, political and economic changes. Czechoslovakia ratified many international conventions on human rights, and adopted a new constitution having a natural law basis. The concept of ownership was again unified and the freedom of business activities became guaranteed. At the same time, provisional amendments of existing legal regulations were adopted, although the ultimate goal was to reconstruct the entire legal system. In many respects, however, such a task was beyond the limits of lawyers educated during the communist period. Since there were some indications of possible dependency on the socialist conception of law, some reforms were being postponed. The overall difficult situation was also complicated by the split of the country into the Czech Republic and Slovakia on 1 January 1993. Due to the commencement of the first phase of the accession process to the European Union, it became necessary to carry out a reform of public administration.

17. In the area of private law, the provisional situation arising from frequent amendments even started to appear as a bearable solution. CC 1964 was being gradually amended on an ad hoc basic, resulting in further fragmentation of its original systemic character and making it even more complicated and inconsistent. In spite of that, its 'socialist state spirit' remained preserved in many respects, failing to respect the free will of individuals. The prevailing conception was that in case of any conflict with law (including failure to observe formal requirements), the relevant legal act becomes void, which had the consequence of substantially limiting one's contractual freedom. For instance, what was decisive for the interpretation of a legal act was only the text itself, even where it was possible to establish that the joint will of the parties had been different. In the area of rights in rem, some fundamental institutes were even entirely missing (e.g., easements established under contract, prescription).

18. In the area of business law, the Commercial Code (Act No. 513/1991 Sb.) was adopted to replace the old socialist economic code and international business code. Apart from the regulation of business corporations, it also regulated – though not in an exhaustive manner – the area of law of obligations including the general part of obligations. It was not quite clear when and to what extent the regulation contained in the CC was supposed to be used. That resulted in many problems when applying the law, which often led to not only delays in judicial proceedings but also some quite absurd conclusions. While corporate law followed the Austrian and German models, it did so without an understanding of the scholarly discourse in those countries, resulting in the rigidity of life of business corporations.

19. It was only at the beginning of the new millennium that preparatory work, meant to address the unsatisfactory situation in that area, was started on the reform of private law. The basic source of inspiration was chosen to be, quite unsurprisingly, the government draft proposal of the 1937 CC, which had been inspired by the ABGB.

E. Private Law after 2014

20. Many significant changes, both as regards conceptual structure and content, have affected the area of private law in the Czech Republic over the past few years. All these changes have a common denominator, namely the return to the 'European roots' of private law. The extent of the changes, effective from 1 January 2014, when the CC, the Act on Business Corporations (ABC) and many other legal regulations came into effect, may strike scholars from other, more 'stable' legal environments (such as Germany, Switzerland, and Austria) as hard to believe and may be difficult to grasp. Nevertheless, since the large majority of the countries of the former Eastern bloc have reorganised their legal systems in a similar extent, this complexity is not that exceptional.[1]

21. The changes brought about as a result of the recodification of private law stem from the idea that private law is not primarily an instrument for the regulation of relations in the society (as was the case during the rule of socialist law). Instead, it forms (and delimits) the space where persons in private interactions may regulate their mutual rights and obligations according to how they see fit, allowing them, as the saying goes, to live their own lives.[2] It is, thus, predominantly an instrument for the implementation of the freedom of individuals, while simultaneously respecting the protection of the rights of the weaker parties.

22. The CC[3] is a very extensive work with more than three thousand sections. It consists of five parts:

(1) The first general part contains the fundamental provisions as well as passages intended for natural and legal persons (including foundations and endowment funds), representation, things in a legal sense, legal acts, limitation of actions and lapse.
(2) The second part deals with family law.
(3) The third part, entitled 'absolute property rights', regulates rights in rem and inheritance. The final section on rights in rem includes the legal regulation of administration of property of another person, including trust funds.
(4) The fourth part deals with the law of obligations.
(5) The fifth part contains common, transitory and final provisions.

---

1. For more details *see* (in English): Petr Lavický & Jan Hurdík et al., *Private Law Reform* (Brno: Masarykova univerzita, 2014).
2. The explanatory note to the new CC expressly states on page 20: '… *It is based on the idea that functional determination of private law is to serve people as an instrument for asserting their freedom. The purpose of the civil code is to enable as well as guarantee the free formation of private life, leaving as much space as possible to the individual persons' free initiative*'.
3. For the text of the new Czech CC see the translations to English, German, French and Russian languages on the website of Czech Ministry of Justice at http://obcanskyzakonik.justice.cz/images/pdf/Civil-Code.pdf.

The text of the CC bears evidence of many of its sources of inspiration. The strongest inspiration for the new Czech code is probably the Austrian ABGB: some provisions are taken over directly, others are formulated in a more modern way, and still others reflect the wording of the 1930s government draft of the Czech CC that was never adopted.[4] This was the base onto which were grafted some rules from the existing CC 1964 and Commercial Code as well as some provisions inspired by CCs of other countries (German, Swiss, Quebec, etc.).

As a result, the new CC is not built on a clear-cut conception that is consistently reflected in all of its provisions. It is, rather, a mosaic or a kaleidoscope of bits and pieces taken over from various CCs. That does not assist in its interpretation and application in legal practice.

1. Conceptual Framework

23. The new Czech civil law, as the core of private law, is based on traditional civil law values that underlie the principles as well as the regulation of specific institutes. One of the most important values is personal freedom. Every individual has the right to live a free life and choose such a family life as he or she desires. The autonomy of a person's will, as the key principle of private law, is thus reflected in the norms of family law. The limits are set reasonably to enable a balanced protection of third parties and especially the weaker party whoever that may be.

The CC builds on the respect of an individual's natural rights, acknowledging the rights by setting their limits and ways of protection. The humanist basis of the code is reflected in many of its provisions. It is evident in the status rights of individuals as well as natural laws linked to human personality.

24. The recodification introduced a relatively extensive general part that is common for all legal persons. This uniform regulation resulted in a significant – almost paradigmatic – shift in the conception of legal persons. The placement of various types and forms of legal persons within the same framework made up of identical general concepts has led to an ongoing confrontation of various conceptual frameworks, refining their definitions and bringing mutual inspiration. There was a shift towards liberalisation and an emphasis on so-called freedom of disposition, i.e., the autonomy of the will of legal persons. The general regulation of legal persons shows some signs of 'commercialisation', i.e., the generalisation of concepts regulating business corporations and the conclusions of business legal doctrine.

25. The recodification has also altered the concept of *a thing in a legal sense.* The idea to modify this category by broadening its conception (in comparison with

4. The ABGB remained in effect in the Czech lands also after the formation of Czechoslovakia. The work on a new codification was started in order to unify the private law regime in the whole Czechoslovakia because, after the formation of Czechoslovakia, Hungarian private law was taken over in Slovakia. For that reason, also the government proposal of the unifying Civil Code was not meant to bring any radical changes apart from some minor modernisations to the ABGB, which had already a tradition of one hundred years at that time.

the regulation valid from 1950 to 2013) initially met with some hesitation and distrust; it may be expected that future application practice is likely to narrow down the interpretation of this concept.

The return to the broad conception of a thing has resulted in several problems that are connected, above all, with the regulation of rights in rem. At present, there is a professional debate in the Czech legal literature[5] on the legal nature of some objects (e.g., the discussions on the legal nature of information, bank account, some kinds of property rights). Rather than clarifying the very legal nature of some entities (and their possible placement in the category of *things*), legal practice is more interested in dealing with the issue of the possible dispositions of various objects, i.e., the specification of rules that regulate such dispositions.

26. Some substantial changes have also been caused by a return to the traditional principle of rights in rem – *superficies solo cedit* – that was abandoned in 1950. Despite some very vocal warnings, the return was relatively smooth. In connection with that, some new legal institutes have appeared in the area of rights in rem, such as the right to construction or regulation of utilities. Major changes have also affected the legal regulation of prescription, joint ownership (including co-ownership of flats), joint property of spouses and easements.

27. One of the major conceptual changes brought by the CC has been the strengthening of *the autonomy of an individual's will* (contractual freedom, freedom to dispose of one's property *inter vivos* as well as *mortis causa*). However, the higher degree of freedom in decision-making about private things is inseparably linked to answerability for one's actions. For that reason, also the conception of legal acts and consequences of faulty acts have been modified as well.

With respect to legal acts, the law generally provides that not every conflict with law renders an act void (section 580 of the CC). Where it does, the invalidity is essentially relative (section 568 of the CC). Interpretation of legal acts is primarily based on the true will of the parties (section 556 of the CC).

28. Concerning fundamental changes in major legal regulations, legal practice tends to be rather conservative. The solutions that had been applied while the earlier legal regulation was in effect are projected into the new legal regulation. Sometimes, the legal practice accommodates to the spirit of the new regulation only after several decades. It is very positive that the above-stated change of the institute of legal acts is essentially respected in legal practice. The formalist approach to interpretation of legal acts is evidently receding.[6]

29. The benefits of the new regulation of law of obligations include the removal of the duality of the regulation of obligations, the approximation to foreign regulations and their solutions and, generally, the opening up of possibilities where the

5. Petr Tégl in Filip Melzer & Petr Tégl et al., *Občanský zákoník. Volume 3* (Praha: Leges, 2013), commentary to § 419.
6. Cf., for instance *see* Supreme Court Case No. 23 Cdo 505/2018; Supreme Court Case No. 33 Cdo 3682/2017.

earlier rigid regulation, which was overburdened with a history of fifty-years of application, could not leave much free space.

At the same time, the new regulation of law of obligation respects the modern trend of protecting the weaker parties from being abused by stronger parties. The law of delicts (liability for damage caused due to violation of law or contract) is conceptually treated in the CC in an entirely new manner from the previous legal regulation in effect until 2013.

30. The current rules revolve around four fundamental qualified facts (violation of good morals, infraction in an absolute right, violation of a protective norm, and violation of a contractual duty). As regards the construction of these issues, there is a clear trend to look into related legal orders (mainly the Austrian and the German systems).

Some of the old (and dated) schemata were also removed. That concerns, for instance, the subsidiarity of claims arising from unjust enrichment (the claim for damages and the claim for the surrender of unjust enrichment now enjoy an equal position and it is up to the injured party to choose which of those two claims to pursue), and the inability to seek damages directly from an employee who acts as an employer's assistant (there is such a possibility now).[7] However, it is not yet clear how these new approaches will be reflected in judicial practice, which often tends to follow in the tracks of the earlier judicial decisions.

2. Absolute Property Rights

31. The recodification has also brought some substantial changes in the area of rights in rem. Most importantly, there has been a return to their traditional conception, as contained in the Austrian ABGB, which had been in effect in most parts of Czechoslovakia until 1950.

Another change in the area of rights in rem concerns a more significant limitation of the autonomy of will. The fundamental principle of rights in rem (i.e., their operation *erga omnes*) substantially weakens this principle. That is why there is a *numerus clausus* of rights in rem and legislators regulate them mainly by means of mandatory rules.

32. With effect from 1 January 2014, several new types of rights in rem (the right of construction; easement was divided into servitude and real easements) and institutes (e.g., ban on alienation and encumbrance of rights in rem, the protection of putative right of ownership – *actio Publiciana* in rem) were introduced. In some areas, the legal regulation was more substantially modified. That concerns possession, which is based on the concept of a possession of a right (rather than a thing), prescription, which enables the acquisition of ownership right also in the absence of

7. Jana Bílková, *Bezdůvodné obohacení v novém občanském zákoníku* (Prague: C. H. Beck, 2015), 12.

a valid legal title (so-called extraordinary prescription), co-ownership, which distinguishes between a usual and a significant administration of a shared thing (and requires, accordingly, the quorum of co-ownership shares of the co-owners), and co-ownership of flats.

33. Substantial changes can be also found in *inheritance law*. More than in the past, it honours the principle that the will manifested by the testator in a disposition *mortis causa* is to be preferred and respected as closely as possible. The range of possible dispositions *mortis causa* has been extended by providing for the possibility to conclude an inheritance contract (sections 1582 et seq. of the CC),[8] and again establish a *legacy* (sections 1594 et seq. of the CC), whereby a testator may establish a claim for a legatee to have a particular thing, a set of things or a right to be surrendered. Similarly, there is the institute of *a testamentary clause* (sections 1498 et seq. of the CC), whereby the testator does not independently appoint heirs but a legacy may be established, a condition imposed upon a legatee or an heir, time postponed or some order issued. There are some other institutes, such as *substitution of heirship* (section 1507 of the CC) and *succession by fideicommissum* (section 1512 of the CC), that enable the testator to specify what is to happen to the property after the testator's death. The code has also modified the position of forced heirs (sections 1642 et seq. of the CC) by reducing the amount of obligatory share of the decedent's estate and by altering the manner in which the property may be sought.

The 'new' law of inheritance is characterised by its extensive character. The relatively complex private law regulation is also accompanied by a procedural regulation that is even more complex and, in many respects, not very satisfactory. Also, the relation between inheritance law and endowment and trust law has not been adequately elaborated.

3. Legal Transplant (Legal Borrowing): The Trust Fund

34. During the recodification, a legal framework for the existence of a trust-like institute – a trust fund (cf. sections 1448 et seq. of the CC) was 'transplanted' into the Czech legal system, whereby the Czech Republic reacted to the development in this area of law in the European (and global) perspective.

At the beginning of the twenty-first century, trusts and other trust-like forms constitute a widespread form of administration of property not only in the Anglo-American legal environment but, over the past couple of decades, also in continental Europe.[9] They are increasingly being used as an alternative to hereditary succession,[10] in the area of intergenerational succession and in the attempt to preserve functioning businesses.

8. Apart from statutes and the last will, inheritance agreement is the third kind of inheritance title recognised by law. Currently valid law does not know this inheritance title.
9. Lately, there has been an increase of interest in trusts and trust-like instruments; cf., for instance, the historicising publication Richard Hemholz & Reinhard Zimmermann, *Itinera Fiduciae: Trust and Treuhand in Historical Perspective* (Duncker & Humbolt, Berlin, 1998).
10. For more details, *see* the following extensive publication: Michael Gruber, Susanne Kalss, Katharina Müller & Martin Schauer, *Erbrecht und Vermögensnachfolge* (Springer: Wien, 2010).

35. The growing popularity of this institute in the Czech Republic (as well as in other jurisdictions) stems from a very simple consideration: while inheritance mostly results in the division of property among heirs and, thus, a frequent loss of value, the property can be preserved as a whole when a trust, a foundation or some other fiduciary form is used, and the property can be used for the furthering of the selected purpose. In addition, the settlor/decedent (i.e., the owner of the property) may suitably set up the rules and conditions for performance for the benefit of a determined set of beneficiaries.

36. The original *common law trust* is, as regards its economic efficiency, by far the most successful institute. It is so mostly because it has a low level of ambiguity and, thus, it is low risk. That is why it has been a source of inspiration for many other legal systems that, while based primarily on the continental legal tradition, seek new forms of administering one's property and passing it onto future generations in view of the current social changes and the demographic structure.

The trust fund is a specific trust-like instrument for the administration of the property of others. In some sense, it is legally unique[11] and its compatibility with the rest of the legal order has not been found yet. It is a normative construction that seeks to establish, in the Czech legal environment (i.e., having the European continental tradition), the existence of an institute comparable with the Anglo-Saxon trust. Its regulation under the new private law follows the main features of the legal regulation of fiduciae/trust contained in the CC of the Canadian province of Quebec (sections 1260–1298 QCC (Civil Code of Québec)).

However, the Quebec regulation was not taken over verbatim. The legislators diverged from it in several respects, which needs to be taken into account in the construction of the individual provisions and in considerations about the transferability of the conclusions of foreign (Quebec) judicial decisions and legal doctrines.

37. The same holds for the application of foundations made in respect of Anglo-American conceptions of trust. They are likewise different, just as other regimes of trust and trust-like instruments. It will always be necessary to assess the overall context and teleological background of national and international regulations, which can lead to different conclusions; at the same time, fundamental principles of operation of trust structures need to be honoured, mainly their difference from (business) corporations and from what may appear at first sight to be similar structures. It is a question of several decades before a body of local judicial decisions and a local legal doctrine are formed, and their shape will depend on many factors.

II. Relation and Hierarchy Between the Sources of Law

38. Sources of Czech law are (in this hierarchical order) are: (1) the CCR and constitutional acts, international treaties ratified by the Parliament, (2) statutes adopted by the Parliament, published decisions of the Constitutional Court, (3) derived legislation: government orders and notifications of ministries, legislative

11. Cf. ss 1448 et seq. of the CC.

acts of territorial self-government bodies (regional ordinances and municipal ordinances). Regulations are subordinate to statutes.

Acts of parliament and other legal regulations enter into force on the day they are promulgated (published) in the official *Collection of Law*, although they may take effect at a later date.

The CCR is considered as the fundamental law. From the vertical legal perspective, the CCR or the Act designated as constitutional is at the top of the system of legal norms. The CCR is a legal norm with a very general content. This requires concretisation by means of the 'ordinary' statutes.[12]

39. The statutes are enacted by the Parliament according to a procedure set out in Chapter Two of the CCR. Proposed legislation must pass through first, second and third reading in the Chamber of Deputies. The approved draft bill is sent from the Chamber of Deputies for consideration to the Senate. The Senate's assembly can then express its will not to deal with the bill, it can pass it or reject it, or, as the case may be, return it to the Chamber of Deputies with amendments. A bill rejected or returned by the Senate must in turn be reconsidered by the Chamber of Deputies, which can approve it either in its original version or as amended by the Senate.

After the bill has been debated by the Senate or repeatedly passed by the Chamber of Deputies, it is then sent to the President of the Republic for signing.

The Czech Republic has been a member of the European Union since 2004 and therefore applies EU-LAW too.

40. Case law is not defined as a source of law in the Czech Republic. Despite that, the decisions of (mainly supreme) courts have a significant influence over the Czech legal system. Findings of the Constitutional Court are considered a source of law, and are binding for general courts.

Scholarly interpretation (interpretation by experts of law theory) plays a particular role in private law interpretation. The scholarly writing is not a binding source of the law in the Czech Republic.

§3. Introduction to the Law of Property and Trust

I. Historical Origins and Evolution

41. The historical origins and evolutions are defined in this chapter §2, I, 2 *Absolute Property Rights* and 3 *Legal Transplant* (Legal Borrowing) – The Trust Fund.

12. Karel Klíma, *Constitutional Law of the Czech Republic* (Plzeň: Aleš Čeněk, 2008), 65.

II. The Concept of Ownership

A. Unity and Fragmentation

42. Ownership under Czech law is the most comprehensive right a person can have over property.

A definition delimiting the right of ownership through its content as the right to control property through one's power, independent of concurrent existence of power of another to the same property. Ownership is an absolute right corresponding to the obligation of other entities not to disturb the owner without a legal cause. The right of ownership is permanent; it is not extinguished unless there is a legal cause for its extinction. The right of ownership includes the right to keep, use, take the fruits from and dispose of the property (legal title).

Unity is a main characteristic of ownership. Fragmentation of ownership is not lawful in the Czech Republic. The right of ownership is a fundamental pillar of the social order, and therefore has its profound institutional significance. It serves as a means of allowing individuals to adjust their life circumstances in the material area. The right of ownership is a fundamental human right and is therefore both institutionally and individually protected by Article 11 of the CFRF.

The right of ownership can be limited by law – e.g., by rights of persons entitled from limited property rights (Part I, Chapter 4).

43. The Czech law includes rules defining the right of ownership and a particular moment in time when this right of ownership passes from the transferor (owner) to the transferee. At this moment in time, all aspects related to the right of ownership (e.g., protection of ownership, the right to dispose) pass to the transferee. The Czech law accepts the *unitary approach*, meaning that one moment in time is decisive in many relations.

44. Although the law does not expressly allow this, in certain cases the consequences resulting from the unitary approach may be contractually modified or excluded. These are, of course, rather exceptions – e.g., in case of immovable property can be agreed that the acquirer will use the item before registration in the Land Register. Similarly, it can be agreed that, after the transfer of ownership, the transferor will use the goods on the basis of another legal title (e.g., on the basis of a lease contract).

B. Immovable and Real Property

45. Immovable and real property concept is included in Part I (*see* Part I, Chapter 1).

C. *Movable and Personal Property*

46. Movable and personal property concept is included in Part I (*see* Part II, Chapter 1).

III. Estate and Patrimony

A. *Unity and Fragmentation*

47. Under the Czech law, in certain cases, the property as *patrimony* may represent a legal entity which will be managed by *trustee*. A trustee has basic power to manage and dispose of the trust property just as a full owner would. Trust and fiduciary mechanism are included in Parts IV and V.

The rules for the management of *estate property* are included in different norms in the CC – for instance in the rules of heritage (Part III, Chapter 2), joint ownership (Part I, Chapter 5), and, e.g., in the legislation on bankruptcy,[13] taxation[14] and execution.[15]

B. *Trust and Fiduciary Mechanisms (See Also Parts IV and V)*

48. Trust and fiduciary mechanism are included in Parts IV and V.

IV. Possession and Title

49. The possession is discussed in detail in Part III, Chapter 3, the ownership in Part I, Chapter 2.

---

13. Insolvency Act (IA).
14. Act on Immovable Property Tax No. 338/1992 Coll.
15. EPC.

Part I. Immovable Property and Real Property

Chapter 1. General Classification

§1. Definition of Immovable Property

50. Law defines immovable property using an explicit enumeration (section 498 of the CC). This can include both tangible and intangible property. Immovable property includes the following.

I. Tracts of Land

51. Tracts of land are parts of land surface usually separated by cadastral map borders.[16] Tracts of land are registered in the form of lots in a public register (Land Register). The right of ownership in a tract of land, however, also includes the space above and below the surface (section 506(2) of the CC).

II. Underground Structures with a Separate Intended Purpose

52. Underground structures with a separate intended purpose are a separate property. Examples include wine cellars, subway or underground parking garages. Such structures – contrary to the general rule that a structure is not a separate property (Part III, Chapter 4, §5) – may be subject to legal dispositions. In the case of underground structures, it is therefore necessary to distinguish whether they have a separate intended purpose. Underground structures with a separate purpose are separate immovable property (cf. section 498(1) of the CC) whereas underground structures without a separate intended purpose are part of the tract of land.

III. Rights In Rem in Immovable Property

53. In view of the fact that the CC conceives property very broadly in the legal sense (property is not only items of tangible but also those of intangible nature –

16. Section 2(a) of LRA.

section 489 of the CC), rights in rem in real property are also immovable property. For example, a servitude encumbering a tract of land is immovable property although it is not subject to registration in the Land Register as immovable property (it is only registered as a means of encumbering the tract of land to which it is bound).[17]

IV. Rights Declared Immovable Property by Law

54. Immovable property also includes rights (i.e., *intangible property*) that have been attributed the nature of immovable property directly by law. Such a right is the *right of superficies* (*see* Part I, Chapter 4, §2, I, C) – section 1242 of the CC.

V. Property That Is Not Part of the Tract of Land by Law and Cannot Be Relocated Without Its Substance Being Interfered With

55. Immovable property also includes, for example, *linear structures* (e.g., water pipes, sewerage, power lines) that cannot be (e.g., due to their placement in the ground) relocated from one place to another without their substance being interfered with.

56. A similar regime applies, for example, to *temporary structures*, which are not part of the tract of land by law[18] and which cannot be relocated from one place

17. This concept has some practical implications. For example, where someone is the owner of a servitude on a tract of land as immovable property, that person is entitled to protection as any owner of immovable property (e.g., protection against unauthorised encroachment upon the right). On the other side, the Czech legal theory tends to conclude that immovable property cannot automatically be subject to all provisions on rights in rem as those as tailored to tangible property. It should always be examined whether the nature of the right as intangible property permits the right to be subject to provisions on rights in rem – e.g., acquisition of ownership (cf. s. 979 of the CC, and Pavel Koukal in Jiří Spáčil, *Občanský zákoník. Věcná práva* (Prague: C. H. Beck, 2013), 1727.
18. In the current expert discussion, however, the question of temporary structures is disputable. This concerns, in particular, the definition of a temporary structure, that is, setting the criteria to assess the temporary nature of a structure. In clarifying this institution, it may be necessary to depart from the Austrian legislation, doctrine and case law because temporary structure originates from the Austrian legal environment. A temporary structure, therefore, will be any structure the builder does not intend to leave on the tract of land permanently, regardless of the lifetime of that structure. The builder's intention, however, is a subjective category and must be determined based on external circumstances. The same thoughts were also the basis for the Czech literature, which is more or less consistent in claiming that the aspect for the definition of a temporary structure is not the definition of a temporary structure under the Building Act (BA), or specifically permission of a structure as a temporary one pursuant to the BA (s. 2(3) of the BA), with regard to s. 1(1) of the CC, under which application of public law (which also includes public building law) is independent of the application of private law (Filip Melzer & Petr Tégl, *Supereidifikáty a nový občanský zákoník* (Právní rozhledy, Vol. 4/2014), 132. One can, therefore, imagine that the building authority will permit a structure as a temporary structure under the BA but under the CC, the structure will be a permanent one, which is part of the tract of land, and vice versa. Another possible criterion that shows the builder's intention to have a structure on the tract of land as a temporary structure is the temporary nature of the

to another without their substance being interfered with. The question of relocatatbility of a structure including any costs of relocation, which will also play a role in assessing whether it is possible to relocate the item, will be dealt with in individual cases, often requiring expert examination.

57. As regards above-ground structures, as a principle, these are part of the tract of land (section 506 of the CC). This is a substantial change in the legislation compared with the situation until 31 December 2013, when a structure was a separate property in the legal sense. Therefore, where a structure is established on a tract of land after 1 January 2014, it in principle becomes part of the tract of land; therefore, it shares the ownership regime and the legal fate of the tract of land. This means that the owner of the structure is the owner of the tract of land regardless of by whom and from what resources the structure had been built. It also means that such a structure can no longer be subject to legal dispositions (e.g., purchase) as it is not a separate property in the legal sense.

58. The law, of course, addresses in its transitional provisions (sections 3054–3061 of the CC) the legal regime of structures built before 1 January 2014, i.e., before the CC coming into effect, as that rule did not apply then and structures were, in principle, *separate property*. Therefore, until the end of 2013, many a structure was built on a tract of land of another, i.e., the owner of the structure and the owner of the tract of land were different entities as of 1 January 2014. The legal regime of structures established until 31 December 2013 is regulated as follows after 1 January 2014:

– Where the owner of the structure and of the tract of land was the same person, the structure became part of the tract of land on 1 January 2014 (the right of ownership in a structure is created by artificial accession).
– Where the owner of the structure was different from the owner of the land, the structure did not become part of the tract of land, but the owner of the tract of land had a statutory pre-emptive right in the tract of land.[19]

§2. The Meaning of the Category of Immovable Property

59. It should be emphasised that the importance of the category of immovable property lies mainly in the fact that in many aspects different rules apply to immovable property than to movable property, not only in the area of private law but also

legal title, that is, where a structure is built based on a temporary legal title (e.g., lease), it is a temporary structure. This criterion, however, does not qualify alone as it lacks publicity vis-à-vis third parties. It seems more suitable to use the criterion of objective appearance, that is, how the structure appears externally (to third parties), whether as a permanent or temporary one, which can be inferred, for example, from the method of construction, engineering and technical structures, etc. This criterion can be probably – for the purposes of practice – regarded as the default one; however, a combination with the criterion of temporary character of a legal title is not excluded.

19. The purpose of the introduction of the statutory pre-emptive right was to gradually merge the legal regimes of structure and land.

in the area of public law (e.g., tax law). From the perspective of private law, special rules are intertwined throughout this area – they can be traced in the area of family law, inheritance law, law of obligations and, in particular, in the area of rights in rem. The following specifics are examples of legal regulation of immovable property.

60. Ownership of immovable property is acquired in different ways:

- In the case of *contractual acquisition*, law requires a written form of contract and signatures of both parties to the contract on the same document (sections 560 and 561(2) of the CC). Moreover, in the case of immovable property subject to registration in the Land Register, a mere contract does not suffice and a constitutive entry in the Land Register is required. The right of ownership is only acquired upon entry in the Land Register. It, naturally, requires that a party to the contract file an application to enter a record in the Land Register, and the entry becomes effective as of the date of filing the application.
- In the case of *acquisitive prescription* of a right of ownership, longer acquisitive prescription periods than for movable property apply. Where the holder has a valid legal title for acquisition, ten years is required, and where the holder does not have such a title, twenty years is required (the acquisitive prescription periods are half-length for movable property).
- *Appropriation* is not permitted for immovable property. Abandoned immovable property passes into the ownership of the state (section 1045(2) of the CC). The law lays down a presumption that if an owner fails to exercise his right of ownership in immovable property for ten years, he is presumed to have abandoned it (section 1050 of the CC).

61. In comparison with movable property, the CC stipulates certain *derogations* or the necessity of *consent or authorisation* to transfer the right of ownership in immovable property. This concerns especially the following cases:

- In the case of a contribution to a foundation in the form of immovable property subject to registration in a public register, the foundation acquires the right of ownership upon registration in a public register (section 331(1) of the CC).
- Where an institute acquires the right of ownership in immovable property, prior consent of the board of trustees is required (section 412 of the CC).
- A corporate agent (*prokurista*) may alienate or encumber immovable property only if expressly provided (section 450 of the CC).
- A guardian may not acquire immovable property or a share in it for the ward, or alienate or encumber immovable property without court approval (section 483 of the CC).
- Court approval is required for juridical acts whereby the child acquires immovable property or part thereof (section 898 of the CC).

62. Special regulation applies in relation to the *statute of limitations*:

– Rights in immovable property registered in a public register become time-barred ten years after the day on which they could have been exercised for the first time (section 631 of the CC).

63. Where immovable property is part of *community property* and it is settled by agreement (e.g., in connection with a divorce of the marriage), such a settlement agreement is only effective upon its registration in the Land Register (section 738 of the CC). This agreement requires a written form (section 739 of the CC).

64. It is necessary only in the case of immovable property to establish a *necessary passage*, that is, an authorisation of an owner to use the adjacent real property for the purposes of access where the owner does not have any suitable access and that real property may not be duly managed or duly used without such access (section 1029 of the CC).

65. In relation to *undivided co-ownership* of immovable property, the CC contains the following provisions:

– Where immovable property is part of undivided co-ownership and the co-owners agree on its administration, the agreement requires – unlike in the case of movable property – the form of a public instrument (section 1138 of the CC). The agreement is subsequently filed in the collection of instruments associated with the Land Register.
– Where a co-ownership share in immovable property is being transferred, the co-owners have a pre-emptive right unless a co-owner transfers his share to a close person (section 1124 of the CC).
– If the co-owners agree to administer the immovable property differently than foreseen by law, the agreement requires the form of a public instrument for immovable property. The agreement is filed in the collection of instruments kept by the body maintaining the public register in which the immovable property is registered (section 1138 of the CC).
– Co-ownership of immovable property may be cancelled only by agreement of all co-owners executed in writing (section 1141 of the CC).
– A stipulation between the co-owners not to request the cancellation of co-ownership for a definite period requires a form of a public instrument (section 1154 of the CC). Where the stipulation concerns an immovable thing registered in a public register, the deferral of the cancellation of co-ownership is registered in the public register.
– In the case of settlement of co-ownership of immovable property which is registered in a public register, new rights of ownerships are created upon registration in the public register (section 1149 of the CC).
– In the case of residential co-ownership, consent of the assembly of co-owners is required to acquire, alienate or encumber immovable property or otherwise dispose of it by the assembly (section 1208(g) of the CC).

66. A *pledge* on immovable property – unlike movable property – is subject to the following rules:

- A pledge of immovable not subject to registration in a public register is created based on a contract, which must take the form of a public instrument (notarial deed) – section 1314(2)(b) of the CC. In the case of immovable property subject to registration in a public register, registration in this register is required for the creation of the pledge in addition to a written contract (section 1316 of the CC).

67. In the area of *inheritance law*, it is worth noting that if the decedent's legacy includes all the decedent's claims, such a legacy includes all claims existing after the legacy has been allocated but not claims encumbering immovable property (section 1613 of the CC).

68. Certain special rules apply in relation to immovable property also in *law of obligations*:

- Pursuant to section 1903(1) of the CC, an existing obligation may also be replaced with a new one in such a way that the parties, by a stipulation, change their rights and duties which have so far been contentious or doubtful between them. In the case of a settlement of a right in rem registered in a public register, the settlement becomes effective upon the registration in that register.
- In the case of defective performance, the CC stipulates that if a defect can be ascertained from the Land Register (i.e., encumbers immovable property), the acquirer is liable for the defect in the case of acquisition of the right of ownership (section 1917 of the CC).
- If a transfer of right as security concerns immovable property registered in a public register, the security is created upon the registration in this register; the temporary nature of a transfer of right as security is also registered in a public register (section 2041 of the CC).
- In the event of a stipulation on the reservation of the right of ownership, the right of repurchase, the prohibition to alienate or encumber, the reservation of a preemptive right or reservation of a better buyer, or a stipulation on trial purchases creates a right in rem registered in a public register, and such a right is created only upon the registration in the public register (section 2128(2) of the CC).
- Where the subject of a purchase is immovable property, the buyer is entitled to a reasonable reduction in the purchase price if a tract of land does not have the area stipulated in the contract of sale. However, if a tract of land does not have the area registered in a public register, the buyer is entitled to a reasonable reduction in the purchase price only if so stipulated (section 2129(1) of the CC).
- There is a special provision on the statute of limitations of rights arising out of defective performance in the case of a structure – if a buyer fails to notify the seller of a latent defect associated with a structure firmly attached to the tract of land within five years from the date of acquisition, a court will not grant the buyer the right arising from a defective performance if the seller invokes late notification of the defect (section 2129(2) of the CC).
- There is also a special provision on the fruits and revenues of immovable property in the case of takeover of immovable property based on a contract of sale. If the parties stipulate when a buyer is to take over immovable property, the buyer

is entitled to the fruits and revenues of the immovable property from the stipulated time of takeover. The risk of damage to the property also passes to the buyer at this time (section 2130 of the CC).

- Provisions on security establish a rebuttable presumption that a plot of construction tract of land or immovable property which serves business purposes constitutes sufficient security up to half of its usual price. The right of superficies, which is also immovable property (cf. above), is presumed to constitute sufficient security up to half of its usual price if the consideration stipulated as the superficies payment is to be paid off no later than five years before the extinction of the right of superficies (section 2014 of the CC).
- If leased immovable property is registered in a public register, the right of lease is also registered upon application of the owner of the property or the lessee with the owner's consent (section 2203 of the CC).
- Termination of lease on the grounds that the owner of the property has changed is subject to a longer notice period than in the case of lease of movable property (three months; section 2222(3) of the CC).
- In the case of lease of immovable property for business purposes, a lessee may not perform other activities or change the manner or conditions of performance of the activities as follows from the purpose of the lease or another stipulation between the parties, or as could be reasonably expected at the conclusion of the contract, if such a change would deteriorate the conditions in the immovable property or be harmful to the lessor or other users of the immovable property beyond a reasonable degree (section 2304(1) of the CC). The lessee may, with the lessor's consent and to an appropriate extent, instal signboards, posters and similar signs on the immovable property where the business premises are located; the lessor may refuse to grant consent for a serious reason. Where the lessee applies for consent in writing and the lessor fails to respond within one month, the lessor's consent is considered granted (section 2305 of the CC).
- If immovable property subject to usufructuary lease is registered in a public register, the right of usufructuary lease is also registered upon application of the owner of the property or the usufructuary lessee with the owner's consent (section 2333 of the CC).
- In the case of silent partnership, a silent partner may contribute immovable property to the partnership – in such a case, the entrepreneur acquires the right of use and usufruct in the property for the duration of the silent partnership (section 2748(2) of the CC).

69. In the area of law of *delicts*, the following provisions address immovable property:

- In the case of damage to immovable property, law foresees special qualified facts (section 2926 of the CC stipulating that a person who, albeit lawfully, performs or provides for work which causes damage to immovable property of another or which prevents or substantially hinders the possession of such property will provide compensation for the resulting damage).

- If a person waives his right to claim compensation for damage caused to a tract of land, and if the waiver is registered in a public register, this shall also have effect against consequence owners (section 2897 of the CC).

Chapter 2. Legal Interests

70. In principle, Czech law as part of the civil law system only knows legal interest, i.e., a right of ownership understood as a legal dominion over property, including the right to keep, use, take the fruits from and dispose of the property (legal title).

A definition delimiting the right of ownership through its content as the right to control property through one's power, independent of concurrent existence of power of another to the same property, has become widely accepted in the Czech legal doctrine but at the same time its limits are pointed out consisting especially in the fact that the owner remains the owner even when he does not have or does not exercise some authorisations.[20]

71. The legal theory distinguishes between the *law of ownership* and the *right of ownership*. The law of ownership is a body of legal norms governing the position of the owner. The right of ownership is a body of rights and obligations conferred on the owner by the legal owner.

The right of ownership allows the owner to dispose of the property in any conceivable way within the limits of the legal order. The owner exercises his authorisations through his power, i.e., power independent of concurrent existence of power of another to the same property; his power is based on law. Ownership is an absolute right corresponding to the obligation of other entities not to disturb the owner without a legal cause. The right of ownership is permanent; it is not extinguished unless there is a legal cause for its extinction, and it is not subject to limitation. Ownership is characterised by its elasticity – once the owner's limitations are eliminated, his authorisations return to the original extent. The right of ownership is not extinguished even where the owner is deprived of his authorisations and is only left with 'bare ownership'.[21]

72. The content of the right of ownership is the owner's authorisations, which can be divided into positive and negative ones.[22] Positive authorisations of an owner include the right to freely dispose of the property, which includes essentially any factual effect on the property such as the right to possess the property, to leave it to another, to transfer it to another.[23] These authorisations, however, are not unlimited; they can be limited by rights of third parties, law, court decision but also by general legal correctives such as prohibition of bullying or the requirement of good faith, or allowed self-help.[24] Negative authorisations of an owner include his right to prohibit (direct) effects of actions of another (e.g., damage to the property, entry in the owner's land). Indirect effects (e.g., construction work on the adjacent tract of land)

20. Jiří Spáčil in Jiří Spáčil et al., *Občanský zákoník*, 135.
21. Jiří Spáčil in Jiří Spáčil et al., *Věcná práva. Katastr nemovitostí. Správa cizího majetku* (Prague: C. H. Beck, 2018), 51.
22. Michaela Smolková in Jan Petrov, Michal Výtisk & Vladimír Beran, *Občanský zákoník. Komentář* (Prague: C. H. Beck, 2019), 1082.
23. Karel Eliáš in Karel Eliáš et al., *Občanský zákoník: velký akademický komentář* (Prague: Linde, 2008), 517 et seq.
24. Klaus Müller, *Sachenrecht* (Köln, Berlin, Bonn, München: Carl Heymanns, 1997), 101.

do not intervene in the 'legal domain' of the owner but where such effects are unlawful, one can defend himself (neighbour's rights).

73. The subject matter of the right of ownership differs according to how the legal order approaches the concept of property in the legal sense (cf. above). Since Czech law departs from a relatively broad definition of property in the legal sense, the subject of the right of ownership corresponds to this (cf. section 1011 of the CC).

74. The right of ownership is a fundamental pillar of the social order, and therefore has its profound institutional significance. It serves as a means of allowing individuals to adjust their life circumstances in the material area. The right of ownership is a fundamental human right and is therefore both institutionally and individually protected by Article 11 of the CFRF.

Chapter 3. Equitable Interests

75. Czech law does not know the category of equitable interests as conceived by common law. There is only one concept of the right of ownership (legal title).

However, a right of ownership may be acquired in *good faith* in the transferor's authorisation if the transferor was not entitled to dispose of the subject of the transfer. In this case, the acquirer acquires a right of ownership that has the same content as the right of ownership of other owners, i.e., the right to possess, use, enjoy and dispose of the property. In this way, the original owner's right of ownership is necessarily extinguished.

76. The protection of the good-faith acquirer and the actual owner of immovable property subject to registration in the Land Register (e.g., a tract of land) has to be sensitively balanced – both of them, therefore, have legal means to defend their rights. A good-faith acquirer is protected by section 984 of the CC, which allows him to acquire, under conditions stipulated by law, the right of ownership even from an unauthorised person (registered in the Land Register), and the actual owner has the possibility to influence the undesirable situation by having a note entered in the Land Register notifying third parties that the actual owner disputes the registered state and thus frustrate their good faith and subsequently achieve the elimination of the discrepancy between the actual and the registered state.

Protection of good faith of the acquirer acting in confidence in the correctness of the data entered in the Land Register is contained in section 984, under which the acquirer acquires a right in rem (e.g., a right of ownership) in case there is a discrepancy between the actual and the registered state from the person who is registered in the Land Register, provided that it is an acquisition for consideration on the basis of a valid legal act (this, therefore, does not concern donation contracts) and the acquirer was in good faith (this is called material publicity of the Land Register). Good faith must, therefore, apply to the acquirer's overall belief in the transferor's right of ownership, and the acquirer must (or at least may), for probable reasons, consider the transferor to be the owner. A certain degree of usual caution that the average person should exercise in the given situation should be required from the acquirer. Such circumstances will often be noticeable in the transferor's behaviour. In this context, for example, too low the price of the real property, disproportionate pressure on the speed of negotiations, unwillingness to provide the necessary documentation, viewing or other cooperation, the owner acting solely through a representative may raise certain doubts in the acquirer. A rigorous assessment of individual circumstances of each case will, however, be necessary.[25] The burden of proving the existence of good faith is not borne, with regard to the legal rebuttable presumption of acting fairly (section 7 of the CC), by the acquirer but, conversely, the transferor bears the burden of proof that the acquirer did not act in good faith.

The actual owner may claim his protection through a note on the disputability (sections 985 and 986 of the CC), whereby the actual owner demands protection of

25. Eva Dobrovolná & Michal Králík, *Ochrana skutečného vlastníka* in Syruček, V., Sabotinov, V. *Realitní právo* (Prague: C. H. Beck, 2020), 32 et seq.

the actual state by seeking to achieve compliance between the actual and the registered state. This can (if there is no other certificate of registration) be achieved only based on a decision to determine the right of ownership of the actual owner; however, until then, the note on the disputability ensures that no other third party may be in good faith (thus fulfilling the condition of material publicity).

77. In the case of facts not related to the register (e.g., the owner is a person other than the transferor registered in the Land Register because the owner acquired the right of ownership by prescription), the acquirer's legal certainty is relatively high because if no note on the disputability is registered, the discrepancy between the actual and the registered state does not affect the acquirer in any way because even if a note on the disputability was registered subsequently (after the acquirer has filed an application to enter a record in the Land Register), the note does not have a retroactive effect. This, however, does not apply to cases where the discrepancy between the registered and the actual state is caused by a registration without a legal ground (e.g., the Land Register Office registers a right on the basis of a void contract, which creates a discrepancy between the actual and the registered state). In this case, the legal certainty of the acquirer is lower because the law extends more protection to the actual owner by stipulating that a note on the disputability also acts retroactively (subject to the statutory deadlines) as of the date of the registration of the right of another (i.e., it acts against the acquirer also at the time when the note on the disputability was not registered in the Land Register, and thus did not indicate to the acquirer that the real property owner should be a person other than the one registered in the Land Register). In the event that the actual owner fails to learn that another person has been registered in his place in the Land Register (e.g., forged instruments), he may challenge the registration within three years after the date of registration of the acquirer's right because the retroactive effects of the note on the disputability will apply as of the date of registration of the right, i.e., also at the time when the acquirer relied on the registered data and did not see the note on the disputability; nevertheless, in this case, it acts against the acquirer and protects the right of the actual owner, who can seek a retroactive registration to his advantage.

Chapter 4. Limited Interests

§1. Usufruct

78. The CC stipulates a servitude of the right of use and a servitude of usufruct. A servitude of the right of use provides the user with the *right to use property of another* for his own needs and those of his household. It is primarily a personal servitude, but it can also be established as a land servitude. A servitude of use can be established gratuitously or for consideration. The beneficiary has the right to use the property in any manner satisfying the beneficiary's own needs and those of his household. The right of use also includes the right to take the fruits and revenues from the property to the extent of the beneficiary's own needs and those of his household. If these needs change after the servitude is established, it does not entitle the user to extend the servitude. However, the owner bears all its defects and must maintain the property in good condition. If the costs exceed the revenue that remains for the owner, the user must either bear these increased costs or refrain from use (section 1284 of the CC).

79. Usufruct grants the usufructuary the right *to use property of another* and *take its fruits* and revenues; the usufructuary also has the right to extraordinary yield from the property (section 1285 of the CC). In the exercise of these rights, the usufructuary is obliged to preserve the substance of the property. Usufruct may also be established with respect to a co-ownership share. A usufructuary accepts all the defects that were attached to the property at the time the servitude was established. The usufructuary is obliged to bear the costs necessary to achieve the fruits and revenues and pays the usual maintenance costs of the property, including its renewal and usual insurance against damage. A usufructuary maintains the property in the condition in which he took it over and pays the usual maintenance costs related to the property, including its renewal and usual insurance against damage. If, in spite of that, the proper use of the property diminishes its value without the usufructuary being at fault, the usufructuary bears no liability for it (section 1288 of the CC). A special provision applies to construction works (sections 1289 and 1290 of the CC) if the subject of usufruct is a structure.[26] An owner may, after being notified by the usufructuary, execute at his own expense construction works necessary due to accident or age of the structure; in such a case, the usufructuary will pay the owner an amount proportional to the improvement in use and enjoyment. If an owner is unable or does not wish to execute the construction work, the usufructuary is entitled to execute the work on his own and claim the same compensation as a possessor in good faith once the use and enjoyment are finished. A usufructuary is obliged to tolerate the work, although unnecessary, if his right is not prejudiced or if all damage caused to him is compensated.

An owner will pay the usufructuary the costs of improving the property under the same conditions as if he was obliged to pay them to an agent without authorisation. If the usufructuary has incurred costs as a result of a hobby or for decoration, he

26. David Havlík in Petrov, Výtisk, Beran, *Občanský zákoník*, 1257.

has the same rights and duties as a possessor in good faith (section 1291 of the CC). When use and enjoyment end, the fruits which have not yet been separated belong to the owner. However, the owner will reimburse the usufructuary for all the costs incurred according to the provisions on a possessor in good faith. The usufructuary has the right to separated fruits and other revenues of the property depending on the length of use enjoyment (section 1293 of the CC).

80. A special provision applies in relation to consumable fungible property if they are the subject of the right of use or usufruct. The user or the usufructuary may dispose of them at will. When his right ends, he will return the same number of things of the same kind and quality (section 1294 of the CC).

81. Money may also be the subject of the right of use or usufruct. In that case, the user or usufructuary of a principal deposited with interest is entitled only to the interest.

§2. Building and Planting Rights

I. Building Rights

82. The Czech civil law rests on the principle that a structure is part of the tract of land on which it is built (*superficial principle*), which – simply put – means that a structure belongs to the owner of the land. Moreover, under this principle, a structure is not a separate property (*see* below) that could be disposed of. Therefore, where a structure has been established on a tract of land after 1 January 2014, it has in principle become part of that tract of land; therefore, it shares the ownership regime and the legal fate of that tract of land. This means that the owner of the structure is the owner of the tract of land regardless of by whom and from what resources the structure had been built.

83. In the case of underground structures, it is necessary to distinguish whether they have a separate intended purpose. Underground structures with a separate purpose are separate immovable property (cf. section 498(1) of the CC) whereas underground structures without a separate intended purpose are part of the tract of land (*see* Part I, Chapter 1, §1, II).

In principle, the owner of a tract of land has the right to build on the land. The law, however, also allows construction on a land of another but with different legal consequences.

A. Structure Established on the Basis of an Obligational Right

84. While the legal regulation applicable until 31 December 2013 was in effect, it was not uncommon for builders to establish structures on lands of another based on legal relationships under the law of obligations, especially based on leases and loans for use; structures thus established did not become part of the land. However, where a structure has been established based on such legal relationships after the CC came into effect (i.e., after 1 January 2014), it may not be possible to count on this consequence. It was mentioned above that it is questionable what the exact legal nature of a temporary structure is. It has been, however, pointed out that due to the absence of publicity vis-à-vis third parties it will not be possible to automatically consider that temporary structures are structures created based on a temporary legal title, which is a lease or loan for use. It can, therefore, be assumed that structures established based on obligational rights will become part of the tracts of land even when they are rightfully built unless they meet (not yet very clear) the criteria of a temporary structure (*see* Part I, Chapter 1, §1, V).

B. Structure Established on the Basis of a Servitude

85. A servitude (i.e., a right in rem) may be used to place a structure on the land of another which may establish the beneficiary's right to build a structure on the land while the owner of the servient land is obliged to tolerate that structure. Such a servitude may also be the right of use or usufruct. A servitude may be indefinite or limited in time. However, a structure that is created based on a servitude is, in principle, part of the land (unless the structure is a temporary one) and it is subject to what has been said above in connection with structures established based on an obligational right.

C. Structure Established on the Basis of the Right of Superficies

86. The *right of superficies* is a new institution in Czech law. However, it enables – with a relatively high degree of legal certainty – to establish a structure on the land of another without the structure becoming part of the land.

The right of superficies is a right in rem in property of another; essentially, it is a method of encumbering a land of another using a right in rem. At the same time, the right of superficies is immovable property subject to registration in the Land Register (section 1242 of the CC). The structure itself is part of the right of superficies (therefore, it belongs to the owner of the right of superficies, i.e., to a person different from the landowner) and it is also subject to provisions on immovable property. That is why the right of superficies can be inherited; it can even be encumbered (e.g., by a pledge). The right of superficies can be imagined as a fictitious tract of land located above the actual tract of land, while the structure is part of the fictitious land and not the actual one. The right of superficies may encumber an already established structure as well as one that is yet to be built. The right of superficies is a suitable institution for cases of refurbishing or reconstruction of an existing structure.

87. The right of superficies is most often created by registration in the Land Register under a contract. The contract must be in writing (section 560 of the CC) and the signatures of the parties must be on the same instrument (section 561(2) of the CC). Any addenda to the contract on the establishment of the right of superficies also require a written form.[27] In addition to arrangements described in the law, the contract may also include other practical arrangements such as an arrangement that the structure is to be completed until a certain deadline, that is to have certain characteristics, etc. It is also advisable to provide for the method of settlement of the right of superficies (*see* below).

The right of superficies may also arise by acquisitive prescription or a decision of a public authority.

The right of superficies may be established for a maximum of ninety-nine years, i.e., it is a temporary right. The right of superficies may of course be stipulated for a shorter period; it must be, however, always clear from the Land Register when the right of superficies terminates. The reason for publication of the last day of the period for which the right of superficies is established in the Land Register is a sufficient publicity vis-à-vis third parties, who then cannot plead they did not know when the right of superficies was going to terminate (section 980(1) first sentence of the CC). A contractually established right of superficies may be extended up to ninety-nine years but only with the consent of persons in whose favour encumbrances are registered on the tract of land in the order after the right of superficies (such an encumbrance may be, for example, a pledge – the pledgee's consent would then be required).[28]

The right of superficies acquired by prescription lasts forty years. If the right of superficies was established by a decision of a public authority, it lasts for the period stipulated in the decision. If justified by a just cause, a court may, on the application of an affected party, reduce or extend the period for which the right of superficies was established.

The right of superficies may be established gratuitously or for consideration. If the right of superficies has been established for consideration and the consideration has been stipulated to be paid in recurring fees as a superficies payment, the encumbrance by the right of superficies is that of a real burden (cf. sections 1303 et seq. of the CC). Consideration, however, need not always be expressed in money; non-pecuniary performance is also possible. The amount of the consideration for the right of superficies will depend on the parties; however, usual correctives such as good morals are applicable. The parties may also agree that the amount of the consideration will vary according to certain pre-defined circumstances.[29]

88. The builder does not have a statutory obligation to establish a structure based on the right of superficies but such an obligation may be stipulated contractually. The builder as the owner of the right of superficies may use the structure; he can, however, only dispose (i.e., to transfer it) with the right of superficies as it is a separate property in the legal sense (not the structure itself). The builder is also entitled to lease the structure; however, the lease obviously terminates upon the passage of the last day of the right of superficies. In relation to the tract of the land, the builder (i.e., the owner of the right of superficies) is in the position of the usufructuary. The rights and obligations of the usufructuary are stipulated in sections 1285 et seq. of

27. Jiří Handrlica in Jiří Spáčil et al., *Občanský zákoník*, 897.
28. Petr Zima in Petrov, Výtisk, Beran, *Občanský zákoník*, 1325.
29. Petr Zima, *Právo stavby* (Prague: C. H. Beck, 2015), 146.

the CC, namely that the builder has the right to use the tract of land and take its fruits and revenues; he is, however, obliged to preserve the substance of the tract of land and to maintain the tract of land in the condition in which he took it over, and pay the usual maintenance work including its renewal and usual insurance against damage. The rights and obligations of the builder may be, however, modified contractually. The builder is obliged to maintain the structure in a good condition but even this obligation can be contractually excluded or altered.

89. On the other hand, the owner of the tract of land is obliged to maintain the tract of land in a condition which is fit for use and to ensure that the builder may peacefully use the tract of land to be able to exercise his entitlements arising out of the right of superficies.[30] The landowner, however, may dispose of the tract of land, and may encumber it unless it is contrary to the purpose of the right of superficies, etc. The landowner may reserve consent with various factual or legal acts of the builder in the contract. For example, the landowner may reserve prior consent with encumbrance of the right of superficies by the builder (section 1252(1) of the CC). Conversely, it is not possible to contractually condition the existence of the right of superficies with a resolutive condition, i.e., an uncertain future event (e.g., it is not possible to validly stipulate that if the builder fails to obtain a building permit until a certain date stipulated in the contract, the right of superficies is extinguished).

The builder and the landowner have a mutual pre-emptive right to the tract of land and the structure. This statutory rule, however, is dispositive and the parties may agree to exclude the pre-emptive right. In such a case, if this derogating arrangement is to be effective, it must be registered in the Land Register.

90. The right of superficies may be extinguished either before the period for which it was established has expired or upon expiry of that period. In the former case, the right of superficies is extinguished by agreement of the parties. In the latter case, the right of superficies is extinguished by law (if its duration is not contractually extended) on the last day indicated in the Land Register. The right of superficies, however, need not be extinguished by renouncement of the right of superficies by the builder (section 1248 of the CC); in such a case, the owner of the encumbered tract of land may transfer the right of superficies to himself or to another person. The right of superficies then lasts for the period for which it was established, but its owner is not the original builder but either the landowner or a third party to whom the landowner transferred the right of superficies.

91. If the right of superficies is extinguished, the structure becomes part of the tract of land. This is a statutory consequence that cannot be contractually modified. When the right of superficies is extinguished, it must be settled. The law stipulates that the landowner is obliged to pay compensation to the builder in the amount of half the value of the structure. However, this rule may be derogated from. It is possible to stipulate a different method of settlement, for example, that the landowner

30. Petr Zima, *Právo stavby* (Prague: C. H. Beck, 2015), 131–133.

will transfer the tract of land to the ownership of the builder, or the amount of compensation can be stipulated by way of derogation from the law. It can be recommended, however, that the method of settlement be provided directly in the contract on the establishment of the right of superficies because agreement on its settlement need not necessarily be reached after the extinction of the right of superficies, especially in a situation where the legal entities can be different persons (legal successors of the original landowner and builder). The parties may also agree that the builder is obliged to return the tract of land in the original state, that is, to remove the structure at his own expense.

II. Planting Rights

92. From the perspective of planting rights, it can be noted that *cultivation of crops* is possible on the basis of several legal titles in Czech law. This right is obviously enjoyed by the landowner but can also be established for other persons.

The first option is obligational legal titles, especially *usufructuary lease*. By a usufructuary lease contract, the usufructuary lessor undertakes to relinquish property to a usufructuary lessee for temporary use and enjoyment, and the usufructuary lessee undertakes to pay the rent to the usufructuary lessor, or provide him with a proportion of the yield from the property. An agricultural or forestry land can also be subject to usufructuary lease in this way. Special arrangements for agricultural usufructuary lease are stipulated in sections 2345 et seq. and contain special regulation, for example, in that usufructuary rent is payable annually in arrears and is due on 1 October (section 2346 of the CC) or that a usufructuary lease stipulated for an indefinite period may be terminated by twelve months' notice (section 2347 of the CC).

Second, it is possible to cultivate crops based on a title in rem – an easement (servitude of usufruct – *see* Part I, Chapter 4, §1).

§3. Leasehold Interests: Chattels Real (*See Also* Part II)

93. Czech civil law does not provide for 'chattel real' as conceived in common law, i.e., as an ownership of immovable property for a limited time period.

Czech law only works with the category of *right of ownership* as an unlimited legal dominion over property including the right to hold the property, use its fruits and dispose of it. The owner has the right of ownership until he transfers it to another person or until the right passes to another person (e.g., by inheritance).

94. If a person other than the owner is to use the property, he may do so based on an *obligational relationship*, which may be lease, loan for use or precarious loan. That person only has the right to use the property and as soon as the stipulated period expires, he is obliged to return the property to the owner. A user does not have any right in rem in the property. In the Czech legal environment, there are long-term leases governed by the respective contract (a lease purchase contract, which is, however, not included in the CC as a contractual type), whereby the owner of the equipment essentially transfers all the risks and revenues to the user (referred to as 'financial leasing'). In the course of the agreed lease, the lessee pays to the lessor in agreed instalments the acquisition costs of the item and the interest costs of the financial transaction. At the end of the stipulated period, after repayment of the stipulated instalments, the ownership of the immovable property passes to the lessee.

95. Another person may also use the property based on a right in rem encumbering the property used. There are various types of rights in rem based on the purpose for which the property is used. First, there are *servitudes*, which enable, for example, to only use the property (servitude of the right of use) or take its fruits (servitude of usufruct) or to place public utilities (servitude of public utilities) or to use a way for access (servitude of the right of way). To use immovable property (tract of land) for the purposes of construction is also possible on the basis of a *right of superficies* (Part I, Chapter 4, §2, I, C). Unlike obligational titles, rights in rem are not extinguished upon a change in the owner of the encumbered property, and it is not easy to terminate them e.g., by a notice as in the case of obligational rights (*see also* Part I, Chapter 4, §6, II, H).

§4. Emphyteusis and Rent Charge

I. Pension

96. The Czech legislation contains a *contract for pension*, whereby the payer undertakes to pay regular pecuniary benefits to the payee (section 2701 of the CC). Pension is a legal relationship of aleatory nature arising from an obligation, and its purpose is to provide provision for life. Pension may be stipulated as periodical payments (fixed pecuniary benefits) or alimentation (the amount of pecuniary benefits changes according to the purchasing power of money). Pension can be used even for the sole purpose of improving the beneficiary's property situation.

It is necessary to distinguish between the (underlying) right to pension and the resulting rights to (periodically recurring) benefits (claims). While the right to pension is unassignable and not subject to limitation, each payable pension benefit is subject to limitation like claims[31] and can be, in principle, assigned.[32] Each benefit may also be subject to pledge and sale in the case of executing, enforcement or insolvency proceedings.

97. A pension is established by a contract for pension, whereby the payer as a debtor undertakes to provide the payee with periodically recurring performance. A contract for pension must stipulate an obligation to provide a pension, and the amount and periodicity of the pension. Pension can only be arranged in cash, not in the form of a fungible property or relinquishing property to be used, provision of services or even transfer of the right of ownership in some property. In general, the

31. The limitation period is three years – cf. ss 629 and 630 of the CC.
32. Section 2704 of the CC.

subject of pension cannot be to tolerate or to refrain from certain behaviour or an obligation to do something (e.g., to provide certain services).

Both natural persons and legal entities may be beneficiaries of pension. In the case of a legal entity, however, it is not possible to stipulate a pension *for life* or pension tied to the period of the *existence of the entity*.[33] The beneficiary may be either the other party (creditor) or a third party.

In general, a contract for pension can also be entered into orally. A written form, however, is required in the case of pension for life or where pension is to be paid for more than five years. The lack of written form results in voidability of the legal act and the associated obligation to surrender the benefits under the rules for unjust enrichment.

Pension can also be stipulated for a limited or unlimited period of time. It is up to the parties to the contract how they will limit the pension in time. However, where the duration of pension is not stipulated, it is presumed that it is a pension for life, i.e., pension lasting for the life of the beneficiary. If a pension contract is stipulated for the beneficiary's life, the obligation to provide benefits passes to the payer's legal successor in the event of the payer's death. In the event of the beneficiary's death, the right to the provision of benefits is extinguished but it is possible to inherit claims that had become payable while the beneficiary was alive.[34] Pension is characterised by the fact that the benefits are recurring. The fact that pension is to provide provision for life or alimentation also implies that it has to be provided in advance (section 2703 of the CC). The law, however, leaves room for derogatory arrangements by the parties, both in terms of the maturity and periodicity of payments.

98. The underlying right to pension cannot be subject to private enforcement proceedings or insolvency proceedings regardless of the fact whether it was established for consideration or not. The benefits, however, can be subject to private enforcement proceedings as well as insolvency proceedings but only up to the amount of the payer's necessary provision for life[35] if the payer had reserved that in the contract. The effects of this reservation are, by law, *erga omnes* although the reservation lacks the necessary publicity; the burden of proof of its existence will be borne by the person who invokes it (usually the recipient). Although the law refers to third parties and public authorities, it is apparent that the corrective of necessary provision for life also applies in relation to the beneficiary's creditors, who can also be considered third parties.[36]

33. This would constitute 'eternal annuity', which is, in the majority opinion of foreign doctrines, inadmissible – cf. opinions in Eva Dobrovolná in Petrov, Výtisk, Beran, *Občanský zákoník*, 2860.
34. Cf. s. 2703 of the CC.
35. Necessary provision for life is the costs of housing and alimentation and, where applicable, adequate clothing and health care (cf. Jiří Švestka, Jan Dvořák & Josef Fiala, *Občanský zákoník. Komentář. V. díl* (Prague: Wolters Kluwer, 2014).
36. Eva Dobrovolná in Petrov, Výtisk, Beran, *Občanský zákoník*, 2860.

II. Reserved Rights of Enjoyment

99. Czech legislation contains *reserved rights of enjoyment* (section 2707 of the CC; *výměnek*), i.e., a mixed contractual type arising from an obligation, which usually consists of benefits (e.g., from pension), acts (e.g., provision of services or bearing certain costs) and rights for the purpose of provision for life (e.g., a personal servitude), obliging the transferee of immovable property to provide for life of the transferor or, where applicable, of a third party. Reserved rights of enjoyment are understood as a special unity of certain performance used to provide for life of the person enjoying reserved rights; since the content of most of the performance corresponds to obligations that may be subject to a real burden (active acts – provision of benefits, services, alimentation, work, etc.), reserved rights of enjoyment can also be established as a real burden, i.e., a right in rem. Provisions on *real burdens* (sections 1303–1308) then apply.

100. Reserved rights of enjoyment are *aleatory obligations* because although the performance of the person enjoying reserved rights is determined from the beginning (transfer of immovable property), a specific period of performance of the obligor is usually not defined in advance – for example, in the case of reserved rights of enjoyment established for the life of the person enjoying reserved rights or in the case of reserved rights of enjoyment established for a certain period with a degree of performance dependent on uncertain circumstances such as the health of the person enjoying reserved rights.[37]

101. Therefore, also in the case of reserved rights of enjoyment, it is necessary to distinguish between the underlying right to reserved rights of enjoyment and the resulting (or periodically recurring) payable benefits (claims). While the right to reserved rights of enjoyment is unassignable and not subject to limitation, each payable benefit is subject to limitation like claims[38] and can be, in principle, assigned.[39]

102. Reserved rights of enjoyment are established by a contract. In view of the fact that part of reserved rights of enjoyment can also be rights for the establishment of which the law stipulates a written form (cf., for example, habitation or a real burden), it is necessary to respect this form for the establishment of such rights.[40] Other rights (e.g., pension) for which the law does not prescribe the form may be stipulated in a different form. If the content of reserved rights of enjoyment is a servitude or a real burden with respect to property subject to registration in a public register, registration in a public register is required for the establishment of such rights.[41]

37. Section 2709 of the CC.
38. In principle, the limitation period is three years – sections 629 and 630 of the CC.
39. Cf. above Part I, Chapter 4, §4, I.
40. Section 2707(2) of the CC.
41. Section 1105 of the CC.

Reserved rights of enjoyment can be stipulated for a limited period or for life of the person enjoying reserved rights.

103. The stipulated content of reserved rights of enjoyment may also include the transferee's right to provide the person enjoying reserved rights with assistance in sickness or accident, for example, by bearing the treatment costs or provision of pecuniary assistance, e.g., in the event of lack of alimentation. However, the obligor has certain obligations of this kind regardless of the fact whether they were stipulated in the contract for reserved rights. These are auxiliary assistance in sickness, injury or similar emergency.

The obligor may release himself from the obligation to provide auxiliary assistance to the person enjoying reserved rights (where possible) by mediating placement of the person enjoying reserved rights in a medical or similar facility (e.g., a home for the elderly).

104. If the circumstances change to the extent that the person obliged to provide the reserved rights of enjoyment cannot be reasonably required to continue providing a non-pecuniary performance, and if the parties fail to agree, a court may, on the application of the person obliged to provide the reserved rights of enjoyment, decide that the non-pecuniary performance be replaced in whole or in part by a pecuniary pension; a court may, even of its own motion, also order the person obliged to provide reserved rights of enjoyment to deposit a principal for the provision for life in the specified amount in favour of the person enjoying the reserved rights with an operator of a suitable caregiving facility.[42]

It follows from the nature of reserved rights of enjoyment as a highly personal right that the right is extinguished upon the death of the person enjoying reserved rights.

§5. Use and Habitation/Occupation

105. In principle, the person authorised to use immovable property (e.g., for the purposes of housing) is the owner. The law, however, enables other persons to use immovable property based on the below.

I. Obligational Legal Titles

A. *Lease*

106. By a lease contract, a lessor undertakes to relinquish property to a lessee for temporary use and a lessee undertakes to pay rent to the lessor for such use.[43] A lease is, therefore, a temporary obligational legal relationship for consideration.

---

42. Section 2710 of the CC.

43. Sections 2235 et seq. of the CC, Eva Kabelková & Hana Dejlová, *Nájem a pacht v novém občanském zákoníku. Komentář* (Praha: C. H. Beck, 2013).

However, it is possible to register lease of immovable property in a public register (Land Register) with the lessor's consent, whereby it gains public vis-à-vis third parties; nevertheless, this is by no means a right in rem. The subject of a lease may be residential premises, for example, an apartment or a house. Where the subject of a lease is premises adequate and suitable in terms of health although they are not intended for housing by a decision of a building authority, this will constitute a valid lease of an apartment.[44]

Lease is subject to special provisions aiming to protect the lessee of an apartment as a weaker contracting party in this legal relationship. Under Czech law, for example, the lessor may terminate lease of an apartment for an indefinite period only for reasons stipulated by law and observe the statutory notice period (three months).[45]

B. Loan for Use (Výpůjčka)

107. A loan for use also constitutes a temporary obligational legal relationship for use but it is a gratuitous legal relationship.[46] This means that the lender relinquishes the subject of loan for use (e.g., housing premises) to the borrower without requiring any consideration. Loan for use may be stipulated for a definite or indefinite period. In the case of a loan for use, the borrower is not specially protected by law as is the case of lease of housing premises.

C. Precarious Loan (Výprosa)

108. Using immovable property for housing is also possible based on a precarious loan but this is a relatively uncertain legal relationship.[47] This is because neither the period nor the purpose of use of immovable property is stipulated. The lender may then at any time request the precarious borrower to return the property and the precarious borrower must hand it over immediately (therefore, no notice period is presumed).

II. Property Titles: Habitation

109. The subject of habitation may be a unit as a separate property or a spatially separated part of a building not divided into units or, by analogy, a part of a unit.[48] The obligee has the right to allow the use of the apartment to their spouse (or partner) and children even if the marriage took place or the children were born only

44. Section 2236 of the CC.
45. Sections 2288 et seq. of the CC.
46. Sections 2193 et seq. of the CC.
47. Sections 2189 et seq. of the CC.
48. Sections 2197 et seq. of the CC.

after the establishment of the servitude; or, where applicable, to other relatives in the direct line whose alimentation would be dependent on the obligee.[49]

110. The very fact that a contract for the establishment of an easement of exclusive use of apartment presumes the use of the apartment by other – unspecified – persons does not mean that persons tolerated by the obligee in the apartment are legally entitled to use that apartment. Such a right would have to result from the text of the contract, which would mandatorily have to be in writing.[50] Where the obligee from the easement has the right to use the entire apartment and unless stipulated otherwise in the contract for the establishment of the easement, the owner of the apartment no longer has the right to use the apartment. The obligee from the easement may then seek removal of the owner from the apartment encumbered with the easement.[51] The owner, however, has the right to freely use all parts of the building that are not subject to the habitation.

§6. Easements and Profits

I. Definition of Easements

111. Easements fall in the category of rights in rem with respect to property of another. They consist in burdening property in a way that the owner of such property has an obligation of either active behaviour (to give something or to do something) or passive behaviour (to refrain from something or to tolerate something) in favour of other property or obligee (cf. below). The owner, however, is in principle not limited in any way in disposing of the property – he may, for example, transfer it to someone else or establish another right with respect to it (e.g., a pledge or another easement) as long as it is not detrimental to the obligee.[52]

112. An easement encumbering property lasts regardless of a change in the owner of the encumbered (servient) property. This means that an obligation resulting from an easement (whether active or passive) passes to the next owner of the encumbered property regardless of the method of acquisition (e.g., by inheritance or contractually). Depending on whether an easement is in favour of another property (dominant property) or another specific person (obligee), there is a distinction between easements in rem and easements in personam. The difference consists in the fact that while easements established in rem are not extinguished upon the death of their owner or upon transfer of the dominant property to another person, easements in personam are, in principle, extinguished upon the death or cessation of legal existence of the obligee.[53]

49. Jiří Spáčil, *Věcná břemena* (Prague: C. H. Beck, 2006), 43.
50. Supreme Court Case No. 22 Cdo 4747/2015.
51. Supreme Court Case No. 22 Cdo 3257/2017.
52. However, this owner's right may be contractually restricted, e.g., by prohibition of alienation or encumbrance pursuant to s. 1761 of the CC. With this respect, cf. Supreme Court Case No. 30 Cdo 644/2002.
53. Section 1302 of the CC.

113. In general, rights and obligations resulting from an easement may not be transferred without the servient or dominant property (e.g., where a servitude of a right of way is established in favour of the owner of the dominant property, the owner may not transfer his right to another person; this can only happen if the owner of the dominant property transfers the property as such).

114. Easements are, with regard to the new conception of property in the legal sense (section 489 of the CC) considered immovable property if they relate to lands and underground structures with a separate intended purpose (section 498(1) of the CC).

Easements can be divided into *servitudes* and *real burdens*. The criterion of division is what the content of the obligation of the owner of the encumbered property is. If it is an obligation to refrain from or to tolerate something, it is a servitude (e.g., a right of way). Where, on the contrary, the content of the obligation is to provide or do something, it is a real burden (e.g., a real burden consisting of an obligation to supply heat to a local hospital). Servitudes and real burdens show certain similar rules but also certain differences (e.g., a real burden may encumber only property subject to registration in a public register – section 1303 of the CC – or real burdens established for an unlimited period must be redemptive – *see* below). The law does not limit parties to private-law relationships in terms of the content of servitudes and real burdens. Therefore, it is possible to stipulate servitudes or real burdens other than those named by law as long as they contain an obligation to refrain from or to tolerate something in the case of servitudes and to do or provide something in the case of real burdens. Therefore, it is possible to imagine various kinds of real burdens in practice – e.g., a servitude may consist of an obligation to refrain from construction and operation of commercial facilities with a certain line of business on servient tracts of land in the future in favour of the obligee's land on which that line of business is carried out in order to rule out that the same (competitive) activities will be carried out on adjacent tracts of land.

115. Servitudes may encumber movable as well as immovable property regardless of whether they are subject to registration in public registers. The dominant property may also be movable as well as property regardless of whether it is subject to registration in the Land Register. It is, therefore, possible to imagine even less traditional servitudes – e.g., a servitude of a right of use of a coastal land established in favour of a shipowner.[54]

116. The rights and obligations that are the subject of easements may also be, of course, the subject of obligational relationships (e.g., lease or usufructuary lease). Unlike the obligee of a servitude, however, the obligational obligee does not have an absolute right (right in rem). This will be reflected not only in the fact that the

54. It is necessary that the servient and dominant property is property in the legal sense; it is not possible to encumber or to establish an easement with respect to a component part of property. It is possible to imagine, however, that an easement, for example, a servitude, will be established with respect to the entire property (e.g., a right of usufruct of a tract of land) but a contract will restrict its extent (exercise of the right of usufruct only to some component parts of the tract of land).

servitude is not extinguished upon the death of the owner of the encumbered property (this also applies to most obligational relationships, where the death of the debtor or the creditor does not cause extinction of the obligation[55]) but especially in the fact that a servitude may not be simply cancelled without a case (unlike obligational relationship that may be extinguished unilaterally, e.g., by notice of termination[56]).

II. Servitudes

117. It was said above that servitudes are easements where the obligation of the owner of the encumbered property consists in refraining from something (*omittere*, e.g., to refrain from building above a certain height) or tolerating something (*pati*, e.g., a right of way). Servitudes are rights in rem and if they relate to immovable property subject to registration in public registers, they are also registered in such registers as encumbrances of that property.

Servitudes must be exercised in a manner that is least annoying for the owner of the encumbered property, i.e., they must not be arbitrarily extended (otherwise the owner of the servient property is entitled to file an *actio negatoria*).[57]

118. The CC now allows establishment of an owner's servitude.[58] This means that the owner may encumber his tract of land with a servitude in favour of another of his tracts of land. It is, therefore, possible to imagine a case where the owner of a land establishes a right of way on his tract of land in favour of another of his (adjacent) tract of land. If the owner decides to transfer the tract of land on which the right of way has been established to another person, he will retain the right of way as the owner of the adjacent tract of land.

A. *Extent and Content of a Servitude*

119. The extent and content of a servitude are defined by the legal fact that establishes the servitude (e.g., a contract). In general, if the extent or content of a servitude is not specified this way, they will be assessed according to local customs, and the extent of a servitude should always be assessed as rather smaller than larger.

A servitude includes everything which is required for its exercise.[59] This means that the obligee may do everything necessary to exercise his right.[60]

55. Section 2009 of the CC.
56. Supreme Court Case No. 22 Cdo 155/2018.
57. Jan Lasák & Dušan Hrabánek in Jiří Spáčil et al., *Občanský zákoník*, 944.
58. Section 1257(2) of the CC.
59. Section 1258 of the CC.
60. Dušan Hrabánek in Jiří Spáčil, *Věcná práva*, 185. In determining the extent and manner of exercising an easement that were not specified by the legal fact establishing the easement, one has to depart from the fact that the exercise must not burden the obligor in excess of the agreed degree or in excess of the degree the persons establishing the easement should and could have expected taking into account the circumstances of the case; *see* Supreme Court Case No. 22 Cdo 60/2008.

B. Acquisition of a Servitude

120. The most common method of acquiring a servitude is *contractual acquisition.* A contract, however, is only a legal cause for the creation of a servitude; in the case of immovable property subject to registration in the Land Register, *registration* in the Land Register is necessary for the creation of a servitude. In the case of other property (e.g., movable or immovable property not subject to registration in public registers), a mere contract is sufficient for the acquisition of a servitude.[61]

121. A contract to establish a servitude should contain an accurate definition of the servient property; definition of what the owner of the servient property is to refrain from or to tolerate; specification of the obligee; term; and the fact whether the servitude is gratuitous or for consideration. Where a servitude is established with respect to immovable property, the contract must be in writing with signatures on the same instrument.[62] Any amendments to such a contract must also be made in writing.

A servitude may not be established if it would be contrary to public regulations; in such a case, it could only be established with the consent of the competent authority.[63]

A servitude may also be acquired by *testament* in connection with the results of probate proceedings. However, a servitude encumbering immovable property subject to registration in the Land Register is only created upon registration in the Land Register. A servitude may also be established by an inheritance contract (sections 1582 et seq.) or an agreement of heirs on the division of the decedent's estate.

The law also envisages establishment of a servitude by *acquisitive prescription.* In this case, a servitude is acquired directly by law, upon completion of the conditions of acquisitive prescription.

122. A servitude is acquired by prescription under similar conditions as the right of ownership (cf. Part III, Chapter 1, §2, III). It is thus possible to acquire a servitude by ordinary acquisitive prescription (section 1089 of the CC), which requires genuine possession in good faith based on a legal cause that would be sufficient for the creation of a right of ownership, and expiry of the acquisitive prescription period (ten years in the case of immovable property). A servitude may also be acquired under the conditions of extraordinary acquisitive prescription (section 1095 of the CC) where a valid legal title of acquisition is missing or cannot be proven and a period twice as long as the acquisitive prescription period expires (twenty years for immovable property). This, however, does not apply if he is proved to have unfair intention.

Acquisitive prescription of easements, or specifically the condition of *good faith* has long been dealt with by case law of the Supreme Court,[64] according to which a

61. Section 1099 of the CC.
62. Sections 560 and 561(2) of the CC.
63. For example, servitudes established in protected landscapes under Act No. 114/1992 Sb., on the Protection of Nature and Landscape – Supreme Court Case No. 22 Cdo 3456/2014.
64. For example, Supreme Court Case No. 22 Cdo 595/2001.

possessor in good faith of a right corresponding to an easement must be convinced that has or his predecessors have a validly created right, i.e., they have a right that is created based on a written contract for which a decision of the competent authority (Land Register) is necessary and that is unlimited in time and passes to the new acquirer with the passage or transfer of ownership of real property that right is associated with.[65] Such possession, therefore, cannot be based on the mere fact that the content of a certain right has been effectively exercised in the long term.[66]

123. A servitude may also be acquired under a *special law*.[67] This is essentially a public limitation of a right of ownership. It is typical of such easements that they have a specific regime, governed by public regulations. Such easements are used, e.g., in the energy sector. The landowner is usually entitled to a (usually one-off) compensation for the establishment of such an easement.

124. Finally, a servitude may also be acquired by a decision of a public authority if the law authorises or expressly allows the public authority to make such decisions. A servitude is created at the moment of the decision becoming final and conclusive or later if the decision stipulates a different moment.

C. Cost Associated with Servient Property

125. The obligee bears the cost of maintaining and repairing the property which is intended for a servitude.[68] However, if the property is also used by the obligor, the obligor is to proportionally contribute to the cost, or to refrain from use. Parties to a contract, however, may stipulate the bearing of costs differently.

D. Scope of a Servitude

126. The scope of a servitude is the intensity with which the obligee may use the servitude. The law usually does not regulate the scope of a servitude; if the scope is not specified in a contract either, the need of the dominant tract of land is decisive. A servitude, however, does not change due to a change in the scope of the servient property or dominant property, or a change in the economic management of the dominant land.[69,70]

---

65. Supreme Court No. 22 Cdo 658/2010.
66. Supreme Court No. 22 Cdo 1417/2001; Supreme Court Case No. 22 Cdo 4089/2015.
67. Act No. 49/1997 Sb., on Civil Aviation, Act No. 27/2005 Sb., on Electronic Communications, Act No. 458/2000 Sb., Energy Act.
68. Section 1263 of the CC.
69. Section 1264(2) of the CC.
70. For example, it would be an inadmissible extension of a servitude of a right of way used for access to a house if the next obligee set up a restaurant on his tract of land and the restaurant guests would use that way for access – cf. Dušan Hrabánek & Jan Lasák in Jiří Spáčil, *Občanský zákoník,* 944.

E. *Competition of Servitudes and Other Rights*

127. In general, multiple servitudes may be established on property, unless a later right is to the detriment of earlier rights.[71] It is possible to imagine, for example, that a servitude of footpath may be used by several obligees. This rule does not apply to servitudes created by law or by acquisitive prescription.

The case law of the Supreme Court has repeatedly dealt with the competition of easements and obligational relationships. It concluded that it is inadmissible for the owner to lease premises used by a servitude obligee to a third party. If the owner establishes a servitude with respect to property already encumbered by an obligational right that excludes or restricts the exercise of the servitude, he must terminate that obligational right, otherwise the performance is defective of impossible vis-à-vis the servitude obligee.[72,73]

F. *Servitude as a Legal Defect*

128. A servitude encumbers a servient property regardless of changes in owners. If a servitude associated with dominant real property (not only with the person of a certain owner) is not mentioned in the course of transfer of the real property, this does not change the fact that this right automatically passes to the acquirer of the dominant real property due to the character of that right as right in rem.

Section 1107(1) of the CC applies: A person who acquires the right of ownership also assumes any defects encumbering the property which are registered in a public register; he assumes other defects only if he should and could have ascertained them from the circumstances, or if it has been stipulated or provided by a statute.

G. *Protection of a Servitude*

129. The servitude obligee enjoys *petitory protection*. He may, therefore, file an action with the court seeking refrainment from unlawful interference with the servitude consisting, for example, of the fact that the owner of the encumbered property or a third party disturbs him in the exercise of the servitude (e.g., in the case of a servitude of a right of usufruct with respect to tract of land, they prevent him from

71. Section 1266 of the CC.
72. Supreme Court Case No. 20 Cdo 1265/98.
73. As regards a simultaneous establishment of a lease and an easement (if the subject of use is identical), the Supreme Court concludes that they cannot co-exist in parallel. Such a 'combined' legal relationship, which includes a lease and an easement of using the same property between the same parties, would only create uncertainty as to what the rights and obligations of the parties to the relationship are, what the parties actually wanted and whether their will was definite (Supreme Court Case No. 22 Cdo 2222/2011).

exercising the servitude by fencing the tract of land). In addition to an action seeking refrainment from interference with the servitude (an *actio negatoria*), the servitude obligee may also require clearing of the property that is subject to the servitude (e.g., if someone unlawfully places movable property on a tract of land subject to a right of usufruct).[74,75]

130. With regard to the fact that servitudes are subject of possession,[76] any possessor of a servitude may seek *protection of possession* pursuant to sections 1003 et seq. of the CC (cf. Part III, Chapter 3, §1, VII). The substance of such a possessory action is protection of the last possession of a servitude against wilful disturbance of a servitude or interferences consisting in making the exercise of a servitude impossible.

The servitude obligee also enjoys general protection provided by means of declaratory action (section 80 of the CPC (Civil Procedure Code)); both existence and inexistence of a servitude may be sought to be declared by the court.

H. Extinction of a Servitude

131. A servitude may be extinguished in several ways:

- A *permanent change* as a result of which the servient property may no longer serve the dominant land or obligee. In this case, the servitude is extinguished by law. These are cases where the servient property cannot be used for the purpose for which the servitude was established. It is necessary that the change occurs without the endeavour of the obligor.[77] An example may be a servitude of a right of cattle path, which enables to drive cattle through the servient tract of land to the adjacent dominant grazing land. If the intended purpose of the dominant land changes (a grazing land becomes a building land), the servitude of cattle path on the servient tract of land will be extinguished by law due to a permanent change because the servitude can no longer be exercised with regard to the change in the intended purpose of the dominant land.
- *Gross disproportion between a servitude and the benefit* for the obligee. A gross disproportion between a servitude and the benefit for the obligee will not cause extinction of the servitude by law but by the court's decision to limit or cancel it. A comparison of the state at the time of the court making decision and the state at the time of establishment of the easement is necessary for the consideration

74. Cf. s. 1259 of the CC.
75. This applies to cases of exclusive use of the whole real property or its part. Where an easement consists in non-exclusive authorisation to use property of another (as is the case of a right of way), the servitude obligee may seek imposition of an obligation on the owner or other persons to allow the obligee to exercise a right corresponding to the easement or to refrain from the disturbance of the exercise of the right specified in the action and to remove its consequences (Supreme Court Case No. 22 Cdo 1856/2002).
76. Section 988(1) of the CC.
77. Dušan Hrabánek & Jan Lasák in Jiří Spáčil et al., *Občanský zákoník*, 1029.

whether a change in circumstances has resulted into a gross disproportion between the servitude and the benefit for the obligee.[78]

The law does not directly list aspects that could point to a gross disproportion between an easement and the benefit for the obligee and leaves the solution of this issue to the discretion of the court deciding on the specific case. A gross disproportion between a servitude and the benefit for the obligee may arise, for examples, where the obligee from a servitude of a right of way established on an adjacent track of land acquires another adjacent land after the creation of that servitude that allows him to access a public road.

On the contrary, where the owner modified the servient track of land and thus created a state preventing the exercise of a servitude against which the obligee could protect himself by filing an action, this does not constitute a change in circumstances that could result in cancellation of the servitude by the court.[79]

Cancellation or limitation of an easement for gross disproportion presupposes that the other party (usually the obligee) will be provided with adequate compensation.[80]

A servitude may also be extinguished by agreement of parties, expiry of a specified period, and death of the obligee in case of personal servitudes or cessation of legal existence of a legal entity.

132. A servitude may be – similarly, in principle, to other rights in rem – time-barred (section 633(1) of the CC). In the case of servitudes established with respect to property registered in a public register, there is a ten-year limitation period if the right can be exercised continuously or repeatedly. However, if a servitude established with respect to immovable property is exercised rarely (e.g., a right of usufruct consisting in taking of fruits that only ripen at a certain time of the year), it only becomes time-barred if the right holder has never exercised the right despite having had an opportunity to do so at least three times over ten years; if, over ten years, the person has had an opportunity to exercise the right less than three times, the limitation period is extended until three opportunities have occurred without the right being exercised.

I. Some Selected Servitudes Regulated by the Law

1. Servitude of Public Utilities

133. A servitude of public utilities establishes a right to set up on or lead through servient land water, sewage, energy, or other lines and operate and maintain them at one's own expense in a suitable and safe manner.[81] An owner of the tract of land is obliged to refrain from everything that may jeopardise the public utilities, and if

78. Supreme Court Case No. 3 Cdon 269/96.
79. Supreme Court Case No. 22 Cdo 3732/2014.
80. Supreme Court Case No. 22 Cdo 1663/2017.
81. Sections 1267 et seq. of the CC.

consulted in advance with the owner, he will allow an entitled person to enter the tract of land for the time and to the extent necessary for the inspection or maintenance of the public utilities. The servitude of public utilities may include a servitude to also establish, have and maintain the necessary service facilities on the servient land.

The servitude of public utilities is a relatively frequent type of servitude, especially in the area of the energy sector, where it is an institution used to regulate legal relationships of energy operators to tracts of land on which public utilities are to be located.

2. Servitudes of Passage, Cattle Path and Passage

134. A servitude of footpath establishes the right to walk or exert human power to travel across the footpath, and the right entitling others to use the footpath to come to and leave the entitled person and exert human power to travel to that person.

A servitude of cattle path creates the right to drive animals across the servient land. The servitude of cattle path is also connected with the right to use any vehicles other than motor vehicles to travel across the tract of land.

A servitude of passage creates a right to use any vehicle to travel across the servient land.

In a particular case, the owner of the servient tract of land may have an interest in not having unauthorised strangers pass through his land. Unless it substantially hinders the exercise of a servitude, the obligee must tolerate restriction of previously unrestricted access through a tract of land, for example, to tolerate fencing of the servient land.[82]

A right of way or of footpath can also be established by a court decision if conditions for the establishment of a necessary passage are fulfilled (section 1029 of the CC, *see* Part I, Chapter 1, §2).

III. Real Burdens

135. Real burdens allow the obligee to require certain *active actions* from the owner of property registered in a public register. This can include various obligations – e.g., provision of pecuniary benefits, certain services, things. The performance need not be created by the encumbered property; it rather serves as a security that the performance will be provided. For example, where the encumbered property is a tract of land on which a fruit orchard is located, the obligee's real burden need not consist of the supply of fruits but, for example, provision of pecuniary benefits. The performance will usually be recurrent but one-off performance is possible too. However, not all active obligations may be subject to a real burden.[83]

82. Supreme Court Case No. 22 Cdo 4491/2016.
83. These must be obligations that meet a typical purpose a real burden may serve – cf. Eva Dobrovolná in Petrov, Výtisk, Beran, *Občanský zákoník*, 1365.

A real burden is a right in rem, that is, it encumbers property regardless of changes in its owners. Moreover, this nature of real burden consists of the fact that satisfaction of payable benefits may be required from sale of the encumbered property, and the performance can be claimed not only from the owner of the property in whose ownership the claims become mature but also from the new owner.

136. It is necessary to distinguish between the real burden as such and an individual right to performance under a real burden. While real burden as such is time-barred after ten years (sections 631 and 632) and is non-transferrable, each benefit under a real burden is time-barred like claims (i.e., in the general three-year limitation period) and in principle are transferable (assignable). The difference between the two components of real burden is also reflected in the fact that a real burden is not extinguished upon satisfaction of performance under the real burden.[84]

137. Unlike servitudes, real burdens cannot encumber any property. Only property subject to registration in a public register may be encumbered. Encumbrance of real property subject to registration in the Land Register is, therefore, typical.

138. A real burden is created similar to a servitude – by contract, testament, decision of a competent authority or by law. A constitutive entry in a public register is necessary for the creation of a real burden by contract and disposition *mortis causa* (section 1305 of the CC).

The law provides that a real burden may encumber several things (this is referred to as a multiple real burden). This may happen either when a real burden is established on several things subject to registration in public registers or subsequently by dividing such a thing; the real burden applies to newly created things.

139. The content and extent of a real burden should be sufficiently defined in the legal fact establishing it; otherwise, the rules on the content and extent of a servitude will apply by analogy (cf. Part I, Chapter 4, §6, III).

140. A real burden, similar to a servitude, may be established for a limited or unlimited period. However, where a real burden is not limited in time, conditions for redemption must be stipulated in the contract establishing the real burden.[85] These may consist, for example, of the payment of a certain sum of money or non-pecuniary performance.

The owner of the encumbered property is obliged to refrain from deteriorating the property, that is, from reducing its value as this would reduce the obligee's security.

141. A real burden may be extinguished in several ways, especially by agreement of the parties (however, a deletion from the public register is necessary for the extinction of the real burden); by expiry of the stipulated period if it is limited in time; by decision of the competent authority; by law; by obligee's waiver of the real

84. Alexander Thöndel in Jan Švestka, Jan Dvořák & Josef Fiala, *Občanský zákoník. III. Komentář* (Prague: Wolters Kluwer, 2014), 872.
85. Section 1306 of the CC.

burden; by death of the obligee in the case of personal real burdens or by cessation of legal existence of a legal entity; by redemption in the case of a real burden not limited in time.

§7. LICENCES

I. Contractual Authorisation to Interfere in the Ownership of Another

142. It is possible to use immovable property of another for various reasons (e.g., access, housing) based on various contractual types, whether in rem (e.g., servitude or the right of superficies) or obligational (lease, usufructuary lease, precarious loan, innominate contract, etc.).

143. One of the contractual types regulated by the CC is a *license agreement*; its subject matter, however, is an intellectual property right, not immovable property.[86] By a license agreement, a licensor grants to a licensee an authorisation to exercise intellectual property rights (a license) within the stipulated limited or unlimited extent, and a licensee undertakes to pay remuneration to the licensor, unless otherwise stipulated (section 2359 of the CC). The agreement must stipulate its amount or at least the method of calculation. Remuneration may also be non-pecuniary; in that case, it has the character of a barter contract. A license, however, can also be stipulated as gratuitous, including in cases where the subject matter of the agreement is industrial rights, i.e., trademarks, patents, etc. The gratuitous character must be expressly stipulated, otherwise the licensor becomes entitled to a remuneration usually at the time of conclusion of the agreement. The extent of license ownership may be limited or unlimited and may be expressed by time, place or quantity.[87]

86. Matěj Myška, Nový občanský zákoník a licenční smlouva k předmětům průmyslového vlastnictví in Časopis pro právní vědu a praxi (Brno: Masarykova univerzita, 2014), 295–304. Available at https://journals.muni.cz/cpvp/article/view/5359.

87. The CC distinguishes two basic types of license, exclusive and non-exclusive. If the license is exclusive, the author must not enter into another license agreement with any other person or exercise themselves their property copyrights entrusted to the licensee. In the case of non-exclusive license, the licensor is entitled to exercise the right it has licensed non-exclusively as well as to provide the license to a third party. Unless an exclusive license has been expressly stipulated, the license is presumed to be non-exclusive (s. 2362 of the CC). There are special arrangements for licenses to items protected by the Copyright Act No. 121/2000 Coll., whereby the author provides the licensee, under a contract, with authorisation to exercise the right to use the copyrighted work in its original, adapted or otherwise altered form, in a certain manner or all manners of use, to a limited or unlimited extent. There is also a special provision for publishing license agreements, whereby the author provides the publishing house with a license to reproduce and disseminate the author's literary work. The publishing house undertakes to print the work within a certain number of days following the author's submission. Finally, the Civil Code also stipulates special rules for license agreements the subject matter of which are rights related to copyright and rights of an author of a database.

II. Statutory Authorisation to Interfere in the Ownership of Another

144. In certain situations, the legal order enables – in this case directly under law – to interfere in the ownership of another to fulfil a particular purpose. This includes, for example, the following cases:

- Under law, the owner of immovable property may be restricted by *public law*. For example, under the Energy Act,[88] the operator of a transmission system has the right to enter, on foot or by car, in real estate of another in connection with the establishment, renewal and operation of a transmission system, to remove and trim trees and other vegetation, etc.
- Law allows landowners to enter the neighbouring tract of land in the event that access is needed for *necessary maintenance and exploitation*. This includes situations where the landowner needs to repair the roof of a house located in their tract of land but the repair may only be carried out from a neighbouring tract of land. It is, however, assumed that they will seek approval to carry out maintenance from the owner of the neighbouring tract of land and will inform the latter of the reasons for which the former needs to enter the track of land. If the neighbour does not agree, the landowner must seek allowance of access to the neighbouring land in court or a building authority.[89]
- A landowner has the right to require the neighbour to allow, for a reasonable compensation, entry in the latter's tract of land for the purpose of *demolition or construction* (repair or restoration) if such work cannot be carried out in a manner other than by using the neighbouring tract of land. This way, it is possible to enter the neighbouring tract of land, for example, when transport of building material over that tract of land is necessary. But even here it is necessary that the owner agrees with such use of their land and if they do not do so, the landowner must seek allowance of access to the neighbouring tract of land in court or a building authority.[90]
- A landowner must also allow access to their land if *movable property* of another *appears on their tract of land*, in order to find and take the property away, or to surrender the property to its owner or to the person who had the possession of the property. If the owner of the tract of land on which the movable property of another is located fails to do so, they may be subject to an action for recovery of property since they are detaining the property unlawfully.[91]
- The right of ownership of another may also be limited based on law by a *decision of an administrative authority or court*. For example, rights to tracts of land and structures, necessary for the implementation of structures or other publicly

88. Energy Act No. 458/2000 Coll.
89. Section 1021 of the CC, s. 141 of the BA.
90. Section 1022 of the CC, s. 141 of the BA.
91. Section 1014 of the CC.

beneficial measures under the Building Act, may be removed or limited in administrative proceedings, e.g., for the purpose of construction of a publicly beneficial structure of transport and technical infrastructure, structures and measures to ensure state defence and security.[92]
- In an *emergency situation* or urgent public interest, owner's property may be used for the period and to the extent necessary if the purpose cannot be achieved otherwise.[93] This includes, for example, protection against natural disasters or industrial and other major accidents.
- The right of ownership may also be *expropriated,* i.e., completely removed from the owner, or limited (cf. Part III, Chapter 6). For a limitation of the right of ownership or expropriation of property, the owner is entitled to full compensation corresponding to the extent to which his property has been affected by those measures.

145. Certain (public) property may be used (for foreseen purpose) by anyone, free of charge, if such property is in the regime of general use.

Such property may be both privately and publicly owned. Property in the regime of general use includes, for example:

- *roads* that may be, under conditions stipulated by law, used by anyone free of charge in the usual manner and for purposes for which they are intended;[94]
- *public spaces* of municipalities such as squares, streets, marketplaces, pavements, public greenery, parks;[95]
- *access to the landscape*: everyone has the right to free passage through tracts of land owned or leased by the state, municipality or other legal entity unless this causes damage to the property or health of another person or interferes in the rights to the protection of personality or neighbour's rights. In doing so, passers are obliged to respect other legitimate interests of the owner or lessee of the land and generally applicable legislation;[96]
- *forests*: everyone has the right to enter the forest at their own risk and to pick forest fruits and brushwood lying on the ground for their own use. In doing so, they are obliged not to damage the forest, not to disturb the forest environment, and to mind the instructions of the forest owner or lessee and their employees;[97]
- *waters*: everyone may, at their own risk, take surface water or otherwise dispose of it for their own use without a permission or consent of the water authority, unless a special technical equipment is required.[98]

146. Property of another may also be used if a person, without being called upon to do so, arranges a matter of another *to prevent imminent damage* (in that case, the person whose matter was arranged shall reimburse the reasonably incurred costs,

92. Section 170 of the BA.
93. Section 1037 of the CC.
94. Section 19 of Act No. 13/1997, on Roads.
95. Section 34 of Act No. 128/2000 Sb., on Municipalities.
96. Section 63 of Act No. 114/1992 Sb., Act on Nature and Landscape Protection.
97. Section 19 of Act No. 289/1995 Sb., on Forests.
98. Section 6 of Act No. 254/2001 Sb., on Waters.

even where no result was achieved for reasons not attributable to the agent without mandate).[99] A similar situation is when a person (agent without mandate) salvages property of another from an inevitable loss or decay (here, in addition to reasonably incurred costs, the agent is entitled to adequate remuneration of not more than a tenth of the price of the property).[100]

§8. Restrictive Covenants

147. Contracting parties may restrict the possibility of disposition with certain property by one or both parties by stipulating a *prohibition of alienation or encumbrance of the property.*[101] In such a case, the respective party is obliged to refrain from transferring the property or it is encumbering with a right in rem (e.g., an easement, right of superficies).

A special case of prohibition of encumbrance is a prohibition to establish a pledge.[102] Under that provision, an arrangement prohibiting the creation of a pledge has effects against a third person only if the prohibition is registered in the pledge registry or in a public register, or if the third person was aware of such an arrangement.

148. The law foresees that the prohibition of alienation and encumbrance may be established as a right in rem. In such a case, it is entered in the Land Register and is effective against legal successors of the parties.[103]

149. In a number of cases, the law directly stipulates a prohibition of encumbrance and alienation as a legal consequence of a particular juridical act; this concerns, for example, cases where property in enforcement proceedings is affected (where the debtor is prohibited to alienate or encumber immovable property).[104] In some cases, the law also restricts or excludes arrangements to prohibit alienation or encumbrance, e.g., in a memorandum of association[105] or articles of association[106] of a company.

150. It is also possible to restrict the other party's disposal with immovable property by making it obliged to refrain from certain activities or to tolerate or do something, based on *obligational* (e.g., under an innominate contract) or in rem *institutions* (e.g., servitudes).

99. Section 3007 of the CC.
100. Section 3008 of the CC.
101. Section 1761 of the CC.
102. Section 1309(2) of the CC.
103. Milan Hulmák in Milan Hulmák et al., *Občanský zákoník. Komentář. Závazkové právo* (Praha: C. H. Beck, 2014), 200.
104. Section 47(5) of the EPC.
105. Section 14 of the ABC.
106. Section 736 of the ABC.

151. Under the law of obligations, the law even foresees certain provisions that can be stipulated in a contract of sale and that restrict the acquirer's disposition in a certain manner. This includes, in particular, a *pre-emptive right*, which obliges the buyer to offer the property to the seller for repurchase if the buyer wanted to sell it to a third party. A pre-emptive right may be stipulated as a right in rem, i.e., with effects against legal successors of the parties.[107]

The parties are subject to pre-emptive right also in cases stipulated by law, i.e., directly by law. This includes, for example, co-owners' statutory pre-emptive right to a co-ownership share.[108]

152. Furthermore, the seller and the buyer may stipulate a *reservation of repurchase*, which obliges the buyer to transfer, within a time limit stipulated in the contract or by law,[109] the right of ownership to the property back to the seller as soon as the seller requests that.[110] Similarly, it is possible to stipulate a *reservation of resale*,[111] which entitles the buyer to sell, within a time limit stipulated in the contract or by law,[112] the property back to the seller. It is also possible to arrange a *trial purchase*, which is a sale with a condition that the seller approves the property in a trial period (stipulated by contract or by law).[113] The law also provides for a *reservation of a better buyer*, which entitles the seller to prefer a better buyer if such buyer claims his interest within a particular time limit.[114]

107. Luboš Tichý, Petra Joanna Pipková & Jan Balarin, *Kupní smlouva v novém občanském zákoníku.* Komentář (Prague: C. H. Beck, 2014), 310–314.
108. Sections 1124 and 1125 of the CC.
109. The statutory time limit is one year.
110. Sections 2135 et seq. of the CC.
111. Section 2139 of the CC.
112. The statutory time limit is one year.
113. Sections 2150 et seq. of the CC.
114. Section 2152 of the CC.

Chapter 5. Joint Ownership

§1. Joint Ownership of Immovable Property

I. General

A. *Introduction*

153. Under Czech law, joint ownership occurs if the right of ownership of one property belongs to several persons. With respect to the property as a whole, co-owners are considered one person, and they dispose of the property as one person. Each co-owner has the right to the whole property and that right is restricted by the same right of another co-owner.

There is a distinction between undivided co-ownership (*'podílové spoluvlastnictví'* in Czech) and common property (*'bezpodílové spoluvlastnictví'* in Czech). As regards undivided co-ownership, divided co-ownership (*'reálné spoluvlastnictví'* in Czech) does not apply (a co-ownership relationship where each co-owner has the right to a defined part of the property). Common property under Czech law is community property of spouses.

B. *Undivided Co-ownership*

154. The basis of undivided co-ownership is an (*ideal*) co-ownership share. A co-ownership share reflects the degree of participation of each of the co-owners in forming a common will and in the rights and duties arising from the co-ownership of the property.

The amount of the share derives from the legal fact on which the co-ownership or participation of the co-owner in the co-ownership is based on (contract, succession, decision of a public authority, based on other facts stipulated by law or based on law, e.g., acquisitive prescription, creation of new property).

155. This, however, does not prevent co-owners from stipulating a different amount of their share. If the amount of co-ownership shares could not be determined, it is deemed they are equal.

156. Each co-owner is a full owner of their share, and can therefore dispose of the share at their will but not to the detriment of other co-owners. By law, if a co-owner decides to transfer their co-ownership share to another person, the co-owner is obliged to offer that share to other co-owners (i.e., *statutory pre-emptive right*).

157. Each of the co-owners is entitled to participate in the administration of undivided property. When deciding on undivided property, the vote of each co-owner is proportional to the percentage of his share.

In the context of administration of undivided property, there is a distinction between usual administration, decision on a relevant matter, and manners of disposal of undivided property that require approval of all co-owners.

158. Usual administration includes matters necessary to maintain and administer the undivided property that are, in the usual course of things, considered necessary and effective, in principle serve the (objectively assessed) interests of all co-owners and do not cause any special costs.

Co-owners make decisions concerning the usual administration by *majority vote*. Such decisions have legal effects on all co-owners only if all of them had been notified of the need to decide and also subsequently of the decision adopted.

If these conditions are met, minority co-owners cannot oppose the decision adopted by the majority. The condition of notification about the need to decide does not apply to situations where immediate action was needed.

In this case, however, a co-owner left out from the decision on an urgent matter may apply to the court for a declaration that the decision on an urgent matter has no legal effects against him if that co-owner may not be reasonably required to bear such effects.

159. A two-third majority of the co-owners' votes is necessary when deciding on a relevant matter relating to the undivided property (this includes, for example, extraordinary juridical acts, significant factual interferences in the essence of the property, especially its substantial improvement or deterioration, change in the intended purpose of the undivided property).

A co-owner outvoted on the decision on a relevant matter may apply to the court for a decision on the matter; within this, he may also move the court to temporarily prohibit acts based on the contested decision. An outvoted co-owner who faces severe harm due to the decision may also seek cancellation of the majority decision in court.[115]

A decision forming the basis on which undivided property is to be encumbered or such an encumbrance cancelled and a decision forming the basis on which the rights of the co-owners are to be limited for more than ten years, requires the consent of all co-owners. This may include, e.g., a decision on the establishment of a pledge, easement or obligational relationship (e.g., lease) for more than ten years.

160. The co-owners may appoint an administrator (or several administrators) by a majority of votes. An administrator is entitled to reimbursement of reasonably incurred costs.

161. The legislation on *cancellation of co-ownership* is based on a general principle that no one may be forced to remain involved in co-ownership.

Each of the co-owners may at any time request that they be separated from the co-ownership if it is possible to divide the co-owned property (e.g., a tract of land), or that the co-ownership be cancelled. The difference between separation from co-ownership and its cancellation consists of the fact that in the first case the

115. Michal Králík in Jiří Spáčil, *Občanský zákoník*, 488.

co-ownership relationship is extinguished only for some co-owner(s) who want to separate while others remain in the relationship. In the second case, the co-ownership relationship is extinguished for all co-owners.

The law stipulates certain limits. In the case of both separation and cancellation, however, a co-owner may not request cancellation or separation at an inconvenient time or only to the detriment of one of the co-owners.

Co-ownership may be cancelled or separated from:

- by agreement of all co-owners, or
- by a decision of the court based on a motion by one of the co-owners.

An agreement of co-owners on the cancellation of co-ownership must contain a stipulation on the method of settlement (the agreement must be in written form in the case of immovable property or an enterprise), that is, division, exercising the power of sale of the undivided property or by selling it at a public auction with the subsequent division of proceeds, or by transferring the right of ownership to one or several co-owners by buying out the others.

In the case of settlement of co-ownership of immovable property registered in a public register, the law links the creation of the new right of ownership to registration in such register.

162. If a court cancels the co-ownership, it will also decide on the manner in which the co-owners will settle. If possible, a court will decide on the division of undivided property unless it results in a substantial decrease in its value. A court may also establish a servitude or another right in rem if necessary to allow the former co-owner to properly use the newly created property. If undivided property cannot be reasonably divided, co-ownership may be settled by a court order that it be given to one or more co-owners for a compensation. If none of the co-owners wants the property, a court orders its sale in a public auction (in justified cases, a court may decide that the property will be auctioned only among the co-owners) and divides the proceeds among the co-owners based on the amounts of their shares.

If a co-ownership is cancelled, co-owners mutually settle their claims and debts related to the co-ownership or the undivided property.

163. At any time during the duration of co-ownership, co-ownership may stipulate that they will not request the cancellation or separation of co-ownership for a definite period not exceeding ten years. If the deferral has been stipulated for a longer period, it is considered to have been stipulated for ten years.

The stipulation to defer the separation from co-ownership or cancellation of co-ownership requires the form of a public instrument; where the stipulation concerns immovable property registered in a public register (Land Register), the deferral of the cancellation of co-ownership is obligatorily registered in the public register.

In the case of a risk of property loss or a serious threat to a lawful interest of any of the co-owners, a court may defer, on the application of a co-owner, the request for cancellation or separation of co-ownership, thus extending the duration of co-ownership (however, by a maximum of two years).

II. Co-ownership of Accessory Property

164. Co-ownership of accessory property can take place in connection with ownership of certain immovable property (e.g., lands) linked, in terms of purpose and place, to the co-ownership of other property (e.g., a way or a parking place), where real property belonging to separate owners creates a unit for a certain purpose (e.g., a garden colony or cottage settlement) and its use is not well possible without the co-ownership of accessory property.

In certain circumstances, there may also be cases that the use of separate property creating a unit is not associated, in terms of purpose, with the use of separate property but only certain equipment (e.g., irrigation equipment in a garden colony). Such equipment (jointly purchased by co-owners of accessory property to serve all of them) is subject to provisions on co-ownership of accessory property with the necessary modifications.

Co-ownership of accessory property in the case of immovable property subject to registration in a public register is also registered in that register.

Co-owned accessory property may not be removed from serving the common purpose against the will of one of the co-owners, and it may only be encumbered in a way that does not prevent its use for a common purpose.[116]

165. A share in co-owned accessory property (similarly in the case of encumbrance with a pre-emptive right, a right of repurchase, establishment of an easement or a similar security) may only be transferred when the right of ownership in the property the use of which the co-owned accessory property serves is simultaneously transferred.

If co-owned accessory property loses its purpose, the co-ownership of accessory property is extinguished. However, as long as this purpose lasts, co-ownership of accessory property may not be cancelled.

III. Community Property of Spouses

166. Matrimonial property right (*community property of spouses*) is subject to the statutory regime unless the statutory regime of the property of spouses is modified (before or after entry into marriage). In Czech law, property community is established upon entry into marriage and the subject of community property is anything that one or both spouses acquired together in the duration of the marriage that has property value and is not excluded from legal circumstances. The CC stipulates certain exceptions where property does not become part of community property and is acquired exclusively by one of the spouses (e.g., property serving personal needs, items obtained as a gift, inheritance, juridical acts relating to exclusive property of a spouse).

Community property includes debts assumed by only one spouse, unless that spouse assumed them without the consent of the other and that they exceed amounts to provide for the everyday or usual needs of the family.

116. Section 1224 of the CC.

167. Common administration of community property is carried out by both spouses or one of them as mutually agreed. Vis-à-vis third parties, both spouses have the status of joint and several debtors and creditors. Other than common administration of community property, more significant matters are carried out by spouses by acting jointly or with the consent of the other (otherwise the juridical acts would be voidable).

168. Termination of marriage (e.g., upon death or divorce) also causes termination of community property, which then has to be settled (divided). That may be done by agreement or court decision. Settlement of community property by a court decision is based on the fact that the spouses' shares in the common property are identical. Only exceptionally it is possible to decide that spouses will have different shares taking into account how each of them cared for the family or how each of them contributed to the acquisition and maintenance of common property.

IV. Co-ownership Applied to Apartment Buildings

169. Residential co-ownership is a special type of co-ownership of immovable property created by the ownership of units.[117] Residential co-ownership may be created where a building with at least two apartments forms the component part of the immovable property (tract of land). Residential co-ownership is characterised by an inseparable ownership connection of a certain spatially separated part of a building (apartment, non-residential space) and common areas of the building and the tract of land, which is also reflected in the definition of a unit.

Under the CC, a unit is intangible immovable property and includes an apartment as a spatially separated part of a building and a share in the common areas, which are interconnected and inseparable.[118]

170. A *unit* may be created based on the following legal facts: under a contract for construction, constitutive entry in a public register (entry in the Land Register, preceded by a declaration of the owner, or agreement of co-owners upon cancellation and settlement of co-ownership in immovable property stating that their undivided co-ownership is converted into ownership of units – this is also possible upon a change in the extent of settlement of common property – and court decision). In this case, a unit is created if so decided by a court in case of separation from co-ownership, cancellation and settlement of co-ownership, or reduction in common property or its settlement.

171. The administration of a building and tract of land includes everything which does not pertain to the unit owner and which is necessary or effective in the interest of all for the proper care of the building and tract of land as a functional whole and the maintenance or improvement of common areas.

---

117. Marek Novotný, Tomáš Horák, Josef Holejšovský & Jaroslav Oehm, *Bytové spoluvlastnictví a bytová družstva. Komentář* (Praha: C. H. Beck, 2016), 15.

118. *See* s. 1159 of the CC.

172. The *association of unit owners* is responsible for administering the building and tract of land, i.e., a legal entity the purpose of which is to ensure administration of the building and tract of land. In its absence, the administrator is the person responsible for the administration of the building.

173. The right of ownership in a unit may belong to one or more persons. In the second case the (undivided) co-ownership will arise. This, however, may be contractually excluded (e.g., in the statutes of the association of unit owners). In the case of creation of co-ownership in a unit, the co-owners will authorise a joint representative to exercise their rights against the person responsible for the administration of the building.

A unit may also be part of community property of spouses, typically in cases where spouses acquire it in the duration of the marriage using resources from community property (and community property affecting the unit has not been restricted).

174. Legal regulation of transfer of a unit in the CC is based on general regulation of transfer of a right of ownership in immovable property. In addition to general requirements relating to contracts on the transfer of a right of ownership in immovable property, the contractual provisions must identify in a sufficiently specific manner the object of the transfer, that is, the unit being transferred, including the apartment included in the unit and the share in common parts of the immovable property.

175. In addition to general obligations associated with the ownership of immovable property, the unit owner has several specific obligations (the extent of these obligations is also modified by the fact whether an association of unit owners has been created or not). The unit owner is obliged to follow the building administration rules and the rules for the use of the common areas if he was acquainted with these rules or should and could have known them. The unit owner is also obliged to ensure compliance with these rules by persons who are provided access to the building or apartment by the unit owner. Moreover, the unit owner is obliged to keep his apartment or non-residential space that is part of the unit owned by him as required to maintain a defect-free condition and good appearance of the building.

176. The CC enables all unit owners to agree (mandatorily in a written form) to transform the existing ownership of units into (undivided) co-ownership of immovable property.

Under that agreement, unit owners *cancel* their ownership of the units, whereby they cancel the legal regime of residential co-ownership and *transform* it into undivided co-ownership of immovable property. A constitutive entry in the Land Register based on the agreement of existing unit owners establishes undivided co-ownership of immovable property and terminates residential co-ownership. The law stipulates a rebuttable presumption that the amount of co-ownership share of each co-owner equals the amount of share the unit owner had on common parts (although a different arrangement is possible).

177. If all units in a building are part of community property and if spouses agree (again, a written form is mandatory) to transform the residential ownership into the ownership of immovable property included in community property, the residential ownership will change to the ownership of immovable property included in community property upon its registration in a public register.

178. If a single owner has the right of ownership in all units in the building and declares (mandatorily in a written form) that he will change the right of ownership in units to the right of ownership in immovable property, residential ownership is transformed upon the registration in a public register.

179. However, if a unit is encumbered (with a right in rem, e.g., an pledge), the agreement or declaration on the extinction of residential ownership is valid only if the person entitled under a right in rem grants their consent also in writing.

§2. Joint Ownership of Movable Property

180. The same rules set out above apply to co-ownership of movable property (whether in the regime of ideal undivided co-ownership, co-ownership of accessory property or community property). There are only some minor differences:

- In movable property subject to undivided co-ownership, there is *no statutory pre-emptive right* to a co-ownership share. If one of the co-owners decides to transfer their co-ownership share to another person, the co-owner need not offer it to other co-owners for sale.[119]
- In general, joint co-owners may agree how to *administer the property*. The general rules set out above on the administration of common property are, therefore, dispositive in this respect. However, a special form of the contract is not required for movable property (it can be entered into orally or implicitly); for immovable property, the agreement must take the form of a public instrument, i.e., a notarial deed.[120] Similarly, this also applies to agreements to terminate co-ownership of movable property, for which the law does not foresee any special form (unlike for immovable property, for which such an agreement must be in writing),[121] and also for confirmation on cancellation and settlement of co-ownership.
- Joint co-owners are obliged to deliver, at the request of one of them, to each other a *confirmation* how they made the settlement if the subject of co-ownership is movable property, unless an agreement to terminate co-ownership of movable property was already in writing.[122] That also applies to community property and

119. Section 1122 of the CC.
120. Section 1138 of the CC.
121. Section 1141(1) of the CC.
122. Section 1149 of the CC.

its settlement by agreement. An agreement on the settlement of movable property does not require a written form (it can be entered into in any form); however, if one of the spouses requests so, the other spouse will provide them with a (written) confirmation how they settled.[123]

123. Section 739 of the CC.

Chapter 6. Neighbourhood and Urban Problems

181. Neighbourhood rights are regulated especially in sections 1012 through 1023 of the CC. These contain a general clause on neighbourhood rights, protection against pollution as well as regulation of cases where movable property or an animal of another appears in a neighbouring tract of land, legal regulation of fruits, roots, trees and overhangs, support of tract of land, construction activities on the land, etc. Other parts of the CC also contain regulation that is, by its nature, part of neighbourhood rights, e.g., the issue of structures on tracts of land of others, determination of land borders.

Neighbour means both the immediate owner of the neighbouring immovable property (or a person using it based on another legal title – lessee, obligee from an easement, etc.) and the owner or user of another (more distant) immovable or even movable property.

§1. General Clause

182. A general clause[124] lays down the *fundamental obligations* of the owner and *basic limitations* of the owner's right of ownership. On the one hand, there is a prohibition of seriously disturbing, beyond what is reasonable given the circumstances, the rights of others, and on the other hand a prohibition of performing such acts whose main purpose is to cause nuisance or harm to others (prohibition of bullying).

183. In general, neighbours may regulate their circumstances differently from the law by agreement (written, oral or implicit). Such an agreement, however, would only be binding upon their legal successors (heirs or new acquirers) only if the law so provided (e.g., in the case of servitudes).

§2. Protection Against Pollution

184. Czech law conceives pollution as the effect of an activity performed on one, typically immovable, thing on another real property. This includes effects physically extending over the property and having effect either on other persons or on property owned by other persons demonstrably negatively (e.g., dust, smoke, noise but also non material pollution such as watching a neighbour).

An owner being disturbed can seek protection against pollution by means of an *actio negatoria*, filed with a civil court and requiring refrainment from pollution.[125]

185. It is possible to defend against indirect pollution only if two conditions are met simultaneously:

124. Section 1012 of the CC.
125. For example Supreme Court Case No. 22 Cdo 4847/2016.

(1) they exceed the level adequate to local circumstances;
(2) they significantly limit normal use of the neighbouring tract of land.

'*Local circumstances*' does not mean only circumstances in the territory of a particular municipality but also the conditions in its immediate vicinity. However, in some cases, the court must also ascertain the level of nuisance that does not exceed adequate circumstances in a particular place but also in a given type of locations.[126]

186. *Economic activity* may be carried out on a tract of land, which may cause pollution passing to a neighbouring tract of land. If such an operational activity (operation of a business enterprise) is officially permitted, it is essentially impossible to file an *actio negatoria* (i.e., an action seeking refrainment from pollution). A neighbour is entitled to *compensation for damage* arisen as a result of pollution only in money.[127] This may include proprietary damage (decrease in the land value) and other than proprietary damage (e.g., to health). Judicial practice takes the view that a privileged pollution is a result of the operation of an enterprise or a similar facility that has been officially approved if the approving authority was obliged to deal with the effects of the operation to the vicinity (usually to the environment). Operation is officially authorised always when the plaintiff seeking protection against pollution was a party to the authorisation proceedings or had the opportunity to object to the operation. If the plaintiff, however, did not have the opportunity to provide their opinion on the effects of the intended operation from which pollution originate, it is necessary, in the case of an action against pollution, examine the level reasonable given the circumstances and the fact whether pollution substantially hinder the use of the neighbouring tract of land. However, it cannot be ruled out that even an pollution originating from the operation of a business approved in authorisation proceedings the neighbour could not participate in will be exceptionally considered privileged. In this case, the conflict of these two rights – the right to operate an enterprise or a similar facility against the right to protection against pollution – should be subjected to a proportionality test.[128]

187. It is apparent that pollution from an officially authorised facility is *privileged* pollution (they have a special status, a privilege among other pollution) from the point of view that no *actio negatoria* is permitted against it (in general, they cannot be prohibited or restricted). Only pollution typical of the particular operation are privileged. Moreover, only pollution that is a result of an officially authorised operation and fall within the scope of official authorisation is privileged. It is possible to successfully defend oneself by means of an *actio negatoria* against pollution that is out of its scope.

188. The purpose of the legislation in this respect is to *protect business activities*, which would be otherwise completely prevented by neighbours' claims. In

126. Supreme Court Case No. 22 Cdo 2573/2019.
127. Section 1013(2) of the CC.
128. Supreme Court Case No. 22 Cdo 4847/2016.

assessing such situations, the case law requires that fundamental rights and freedoms be considered and examined from the point of view of a proportionality test. On the one hand, there is an interest in the development of business activities and the right of ownership of the enterprise owner, and on the other hand, there is *protection of health and lives of inhabitants* as well as protection of the environment and the proprietary right of the neighbour.

189. From this point of view, it is always necessary to consider whether and what measures the enterprise operator takes to prevent pollution. This is because an *actio negatoria* against nuisance by privileged pollution may be disposed of affirmatively, *inter alia*, only when pollution can be prevented by a technical or organisational measure that will not disproportionately burden the operator and can be reasonably required from the operator.

190. A special problem is pollution *caused by traffic on public roads.* In practice, a question arises whether also roads are an officially authorised facility or how to assess pollution originating from the general use of roads (noise, dustiness, etc.). It is argued that traffic on roads in relation to pollution from general usage is not an officially authorised facility.[129]

191. As regards road traffic, judicial practice distinguishes two groups of cases:

(1) Pollution resulting from the construction condition or transport and technical condition of roads; in these cases the court proceeds as follows. It determines:
   - whether the nuisance goes beyond what is reasonable given the circumstances and whether it restricts normal use of real property (i.e., similar real property by similar roads), and will take into account whether pollution causing nuisance to the plaintiff exceed limits stipulated in public regulations (these limits, however, are only an auxiliary, albeit significant indicator);
   - whether the pollutions that cause nuisance to the plaintiff originate at least partly in the construction condition of the road (or in other circumstances attributable to the defendant, e.g., in the frequency and quality of road cleaning) and whether they can be influenced by its modifications (taking into account the costs of sound protection or other measures and their contribution to reducing the plaintiff's noise burden).

   If the court concludes that both assumptions are met, it will oblige the defendant to refrain from pollution; the grounds of the decision will state what defects need to be remedied to prevent or reduce pollution, and may also state what measures should be taken.
(2) Noise pollutions from road traffic – the question of nuisance by pollution from general use of roads is significantly influenced by the fact that the road owner (e.g., a municipality in the case of a local road) is obliged to tolerate general use of that road without a considerable possibility to regulate traffic on it. In

129. Supreme Court Case No. 22 Cdo 3277/2014.

such cases, a proportionality test is used. The court considers the extent of protected interest(s), intensity of nuisance, consequences of pollution load, objective possibilities to prevent nuisance by pollution, etc. It is also examined whether – with regard to factual real possibilities – the road owner carries out adequate organisational and technical measures to reduce pollution, namely, for example, by building a noise protection wall or by modifying window structures.[130] A strict individual assessment may lead, in some cases, to protection of interests of a person seeking judicial intervention against nuisance by pollution, and in some cases to action dismissal.

§3. Trees, Shrubs and Fruits

192. *Overhangs* (branches extending over a neighbouring tract of land) and *tree roots* may have negative effects on the neighbouring tract of land (e.g., shadowing, falling leaves, drainage of moisture and nutrients).

The landowner is entitled to remove tree roots or branches extending over the owner's tract of land; however, only if they cause damage to the owner (e.g., cracking of a wall on a construction site) or other difficulties exceeding the interest on intact preservation of the tree. A precondition of *self-help intervention* of removal of tree roots or branches is a neighbour's request for their removal; only if the tree owner fails to remove the roots within a reasonable time, the bothered landowner is entitled to remove them.

193. As regards the ownership of *fruits* fallen from trees and shrubs, fruits spontaneously fallen on a neighbouring tract of land belong to the owner of the neighbouring tract of land.

194. The CC also contains legal regulation of *planting trees* in close proximity to the border, which may cause considerable difficulties to neighbours. If an owner of a tract of land has a reasonable cause, he may require a neighbour to refrain from planting trees near the common border of the tracts of land and to remove them where the neighbour has already planted the trees or let them grow. The owner may also make a judicial claim in that respect.[131]

§4. Construction and Economic Activities on a Tract of Land

195. A landowner may defend himself against establishment of a construction on a neighbouring tract of land if the structure is being established adjacent to the common border of the tracts of land (e.g., if he is afraid of shadow pollution).[132] A land owner may also place a fence on his property.

130. Supreme Court Case No. 22 Cdo 3559/2012.
131. Section 1017 of the CC.
132. Section 1020 of the CC.

§5. A Thing on a Tract of Land of Another

196. Generally, a landowner is in principle obliged to prevent entry of his *movable things or animals* in the neighbouring land. A repeated entry of movable things or animals may be considered pollution, which can be contested by an *actio negatoria*.

197. When lands are used, a thing or an animal may enter a neighbouring tract of land. In such a case, the law obliges the neighbour to surrender the thing or bred animal to its owner or, if he fails to surrender it himself, to allow the owner to find the thing or animal and take it away.[133] Otherwise, the owner of the movable thing or bred animal could file an action for its recovery.

198. A thing or a bred animal on a neighbouring land may cause damage. In these cases, the landowner is entitled to compensation for damage[134] as well as to a retention right (if a movable thing caused damage on the tract of land of another, the landowner may retain the thing until he receives other security or compensation for the damage[135]) until the owner of the thing or bred animal provides him with other security (e.g., establishes a pledge to other property as security). In the case of retention, however, the landowner is obliged to inform the owner of the thing or animal and to administer them with due managerial care; he may use them only with the consent of the owner of the thing or animal and in a manner which is harmless for the debtor.[136]

133. Section 1014 of the CC.
134. Section 1014(2) and s. 2910 of the CC.
135. Section 1015 of the CC.
136. Section 1397 of the CC.

Chapter 7. Agrarian Problems

199. Agriculture plays a vital role in the Czech national economy. Agricultural land accounts for 54% of the territory of the Czech Republic. The size of agricultural land is steadily declining in favour of forest land and built-up and other areas. The acreage of arable land is decreasing in favour of permanent grassland. As regards the ownership structure of agricultural land, it is mostly owned privately by natural persons (76%) and legal entities (20%). State-owned land accounts only for 3.5%. Legal entities use lease or usufructuary lease relationships for the management of agricultural land.

200. Land is perceived in two perspectives, an economic one, when it is considered an area necessary for economic or other activity, and an environmental one, which means that land is a retention space for water and ensures its circulation in nature, captures solar energy, stores carbon from the air, is a reservoir of raw materials, and other natural wealth.[137]

201. As regards the market price of agricultural land, it is constantly increasing, which leads to various attempts to regulate the land market, for the time being in the form of bills. The economically decisive part of Czech agriculture is of a large-scale production character with a predominance of hired work and land, and with a relatively low degree of diversification of activities. These characteristics do create a potential profit from the economies of scale, but on the other hand, they reduce the room for manoeuvre in risk management, in some cases worsen the relationships to environmentally friendly use of land, and in the case of a decline in more labour-intensive production do not contribute to maintaining rural employment.[138]

202. The aim of legislation on agriculture in the Czech Republic is to provide basic nutrition for inhabitants, food security and necessary non-food raw materials as well as free movement of agricultural products, protection of environmental components such as land, water and air, and to maintain populated and cultural landscape. It also aims to develop diverse economic activities and improve the quality of life in rural areas, and to develop villages.

203. Agricultural law also includes legal regulations governing legal relationships in the context of agricultural activities. These include private as well as public regulations. Legal protection of land is contained in many special legal regulations; uniform regulation applies especially to the area of agricultural land resources[139] and forest land.[140] From the perspective of private law (disposal of agricultural land), the general regulation of disposal of immovable property contained in the CC will be used in principle. There are only a few differences – for example, where an

137. Milan Damohorský, *Právo životního prostředí. 3th edition* (Praha: C. H. Beck, 2010), 31.
138. Ministry of Agriculture Strategy till 2030. Available at http://eagri.cz/public/web/file/538509/Strategie_MZe_final_s_grafikou.pdf.
139. Act No. 334/1992 Sb., on the Protection of Agricultural Land Resources.
140. Act No. 289/1995 Sb., on Forests.

agricultural tract of land is in an undivided co-ownership, it may only be divided in a way that it results in the creation of tracts of land which may be efficiently cultivated both in terms of their amount, as well as the possibility of permanent access.[141] There is also a restriction with respect to forest lands, namely in relation to servitudes – it is possible to establish only some servitudes, which, in addition, must be redemptive, i.e., a manner of their extinguishment must be agreed according to which a servitude is extinguished upon fulfilment of the stipulated conditions are met (e.g., payment of a certain pecuniary amount).[142]

141. Section 1142(2) of the CC.
142. Section 1261 of the CC.

Part II. Movable Property and Personal Property/Chattels

Chapter 1. General Classification

§1. Tangible Movable Property and Choses in Possession

204. The law defines the term '*movable property*' as property that is not immovable.[143] For the definition of immovable property cf. Part I, Chapter 1, §1.

205. An indicative aspect is that movable property may be carried from one place to another without damage. Tangible movable property is a controllable and separate piece of matter.[144] The characteristic of controllability is not met, e.g., by air or sunlight, which are therefore not property. A mere part of property or component of property (e.g., car bodywork) does not meet the characteristic of separateness and, therefore, is not itself property.[145] In general, a component of property is everything that pertains to the property by its nature and cannot be separated without devaluating it.[146]

206. The provisions on tangible property will also apply to *controllable forces of nature* (section 497 of the CC) but only with necessary modifications, i.e., to the extent to which this is proportionate to the character of the controllable force of nature and the matter under assessment.

§2. Intangible Movable Property and Choses in Action

207. As conceived by Czech law, many intangible things are movable properties. This is because Czech law has a broad definition of property in a legal sense – it considers property as everything that is different from a person and serves the needs of people.[147]

143. Section 498(2) of the CC.
144. Emanuel Tilsch, *Občanské právo. Část všeobecná* (Prague: Wolters Kluwer, 1925, reprint 2012), p. 143.
145. Jan Petrov in Jiří Spáčil, *Věcná práva*, 13.
146. Section 505 of the CC.
147. Section 489 of the CC.

208. Therefore, intangible movable property includes, for example, *industrial rights* (patents or trademarks), which are created under special laws.[148] It can also include *book-entry securities* (sections 525 et seq. of the CC[149]), e.g., *book-entry shares*, which are created and are represented by an entry in the relevant electronic account. Intangible movable property is also a share in business companies such as a share of a member in a limited-liability company.

Intangible property forms a substantially less homogeneous group than tangible property. It is of different nature and quality and is governed primarily by special provisions of the CC or special laws.[150]

209. According to the literature,[151] only property rights that are transferable and allow permanent or repeated exercise may be subject to ownership; this is presumably based on the fact that rights that cannot be subject to possession because they do not allow such exercise may not be subject to ownership either. 'Ownership' as defined in the CC covers two basic groups of subjects – tangible and intangible property – and based on these it divides the concept of 'right of ownership' into two categories: right of ownership in a broader sense, covering tangible as well as intangible property, and right of ownership in a narrower sense involving only tangible property. This is because most provisions of the CC on rights in rem are only suitable for the nature of tangible property (e.g., an action for recovery of property, protection against pollution); the nature of intangible property does not allow application of these provisions.

210. Intangible movable property exhibits such strong specificities that the Czech legal doctrine deals with it in special subdisciplines – e.g., industrial property law, book-entry securities law, law or corporations or competition law.

§3. Funds (Capital; Investment Fund)

211. Under Czech law, property (intangible) includes money (notes) and in general also investment instruments. In view of the fact that this concept of property in a legal sense has applied in the Czech Republic only since 1 January 2014, case law has not dealt with such property in terms of rights in rem, and the literature does not contain any comprehensive treatises.

212. Under capital market law, investment instruments are investment securities, collective investment securities, money market instruments, and derivatives. As regards investment securities, they are defined as securities that can be traded on the capital market. Collective investment securities are especially investment fund

148. For example, Act No. 527/1990 Coll., on Inventions and Rationalisation Proposals, or Act No. 441/2003 Coll., on Trademarks.

149. Radan Marek & Václav Ježek, *Cenné papíry v novém občanském zákoníku. Komentář* (Prague: C. H. Beck, 2013), 52–61.

150. For example, trademarks are governed by the Trademark Act No. 441/2003 Coll, etc.

151. Alexander Thöndel in Jan Švestka, Jan Dvořák, Josef Fiala, *Občanský zákoník. III. Komentář* (Prague: Wolters Kluwer, 2014), 8.

shares and mutual funds certificates. Money market instruments include short-term and long-term loans, commercial papers, certificates of deposit, and bills of deposit.

213. Czech law knows investment funds as a way to invest money as part of a group together with other investors in order to benefit financially. Under Czech law, an investment fund is a legal entity, which can take various legal forms. Most often, it is a joint-stock company which obtains funds for investment from subscriptions of shares purchased by investors (therefore, investors are shareholders). Investment funds in the Czech Republic are governed by a special law, Act No. 240/2013 Sb., on Investment Companies and Investment Funds (ICIF).

214. The legislation does not distinguish between collective investment funds and qualifying investor funds.

A mutual fund or a joint-stock company may be a collective investment fund.

A joint-stock company may collect funds from the public by issuing shares and subsequently invest the money based on an investment strategy on the principle of distribution of risk for the benefit of the share owners; it also provides management of such assets. A mutual fund is established in order to collect funds from the public by issuing mutual fund certificates and investing the collected funds based on an investment strategy on the principle of distribution of risk for the benefit of the mutual fund owners; it also provides management of such assets.

215. Qualifying investor funds are legal entities based in the Czech Republic entitled to collect funds or property valuable by money from several qualifying investors – by issuing participating securities or by qualifying investors becoming its members and subsequently investing jointly the collected funds or property valuable by money based on an investment strategy on the principle of distribution of risk for the benefit of the qualifying investors; they also provide management of such assets. Qualifying investor funds include trusts, limited partnership companies, limited-liability companies, European Companies (Societas Europaea) and cooperatives.

§4. CHATTELS PERSONAL AND CHATTELS REAL (*SEE ALSO* PART I)

216. Czech civil law does not provide for 'chattel real' as conceived in common law, i.e., as an ownership of immovable property for a limited time period.

Czech law only works with the category of right of ownership as an *unlimited legal dominion over property* including the right to hold the property, use its fruits and dispose of it. The owner has the right of ownership until he transfers it to another person or until the right passes to another person (e.g., by inheritance).

217. If a person other than the owner is to use the property, he may do so based on an obligational relationship or a right in rem (*see* Part I).

Chapter 2. Legal Interests

218. In principle, Czech law as part of the civil law system only knows legal interest, i.e., a right of ownership understood as a legal dominion over property, including the right to keep, use, take the fruits from and dispose of the property (legal title) – cf. the explanation in Part I, Chapter 2, which applies equally to movable property.

Chapter 3. Equitable Interests

219. Czech law does not know the category of equitable interests as conceived by common law. There is only one concept of the right of ownership (legal title).

220. However, a right of ownership may be acquired in *good faith* in the transferor's authorisation if the transferor was not entitled to dispose of the subject of the transfer. In this case, the acquirer acquires a right of ownership that has the same content as the right of ownership of other owners, i.e., the right to possess, use, enjoy and dispose of the property. In this way, the original owner's right of ownership is necessarily extinguished.

221. Right of ownership in movable property from a non-entitled person is acquired immediately, i.e., upon accomplishment of statutory conditions for acquisition of ownership – except the transferor's authorisation (therefore, this is not an acquisitive prescription, where a right of ownership is acquired by long-term possession if other conditions are met).

222. General prerequisites of acquisition of movable property from a non-entitled person are a valid legal title of acquisition and the acquirer's good faith.

The prerequisite of validity of the legal title of acquisition is justified by the fact that the institution of acquisition from a non-entitled person should not rehabilitate defects of a legal title of acquisition but only missing authorisation of the transferor. Therefore, if the legal title of acquisition (contract) has a legal defect, i.e., it is void for the lack of legal capacity, acquisition from a non-entitled person may not take place because acquisition from an entitled person would not take place either in such a case.[152]

In addition to a validly concluded contract, it is necessary that other statutory conditions for the completion of transfer of a right of ownership are met. In the case of movable property, the law does not require handover of property (unless it has been stipulated), but it is necessary to insist on it because it is an important indication of the acquirer's good faith.

Good faith as another prerequisite for acquisition from a non-entitled person represents subjective and objective belief of the acquirer that the transferor had a right of ownership. When examining the acquirer's good faith, one should take into account the degree of usual caution that may be required from the average person in a given situation.[153]

223. Further conditions for acquisition from a non-entitled person are set out below.

It is not possible to acquire property from a non-entitled person that was stolen from its owner or lost by the owner.

---

152. Cf. s. 1760 of the CC, pursuant to which a lack of authorisation of the transferor does not invalidate the contract.
153. Supreme Court Case No. 22 Cdo 877/2009.

224. In addition to the aforementioned basic general rule, the legislation also contains special rule, i.e., privileged facts of acquisition from a non-entitled person.[154] Such facts are called privileged because they allow acquisition of property stolen from the owner or lost by the owner and because the proof of burden is distributed differently than in the case of the general rule – it is not borne by the acquirer in terms of existence of good faith but the original owner has the burden of proof of its inexistence.

225. These privileged methods of acquisition are:

- acquisition at a public auction;
- acquisition from an entrepreneur in his business activities in the ordinary course of business;
- acquisition for a reward from a person to whom the owner entrusted the thing;
- acquisition from an unlawful heir, whose acquisition of inheritance has been confirmed;
- acquisition when trading with an investment instrument, security or instrument made out to the bearer; or
- acquisition when trading at the commodity exchange.

226. In addition, the CC also foresees another special fact, which is acquisition from a non-entitled person in good faith in the case of movable used property from an entrepreneur who trades in such property in the ordinary course of trade as part of their business. However, acquisition of stolen or lost property is excluded here.[155]

Acquisition of a right of ownership by a person knowing that their legal predecessor had acquired the right of ownership from a non-entitled person is also excluded.[156] This should prevent anyone from benefiting from their own unlawful conduct.

154. Section 1109 of the CC.
155. Eva Dobrovolná in Jiří Spáčil et al., *Občanský zákoník*, 377.
156. Section 1112 of the CC.

Chapter 4. Security Interests (*See Also* Parts I, IV, and V)

227. Movable property may be subject to security. Most often, these are in rem methods of security such as pledge or retention right. These (and other) security institutions are dealt with in more detail in relation to movable property (Part V).

Part III. Acquisition of Property Rights

Chapter 1. Transfer of Property by Contract *Inter Vivos*

§1. Introduction

228. A transfer of a right of ownership is a derivative means of acquisition, that is, one at the will of the previous owner.

The requirements for the acquisition of rights in rem stipulated by law as well as the moment of acquisition of rights in rem differ depending on whether rights in rem are acquired with respect to movable property, immovable property or property subject to registration or not subject to registration in public registers, or whether a right of ownership is acquired from an entitled or non-entitled person. In principle, the conditions for the acquisition of rights in rem in immovable property – unlike acquisition of rights in rem in movable property – are stipulated more strictly (e.g., a requirement of a written form of the legal act in case of contractual establishment of a right in rem – sections 560 and 561(2) of the CC).

§2. Prerequisites of a Transfer of a Right of Ownership

229. A transfer of a right of ownership is its acquisition *based on a contract* that leads to the acquisition of the right of ownership (a transfer contract, legal title of acquisition, *titulus*), which may be a contract of sale, donation or exchange.

Depending on the circumstances of the transfer, what property is subject to transfer and whether it is subject to registration in a public register or not, such a contract either establishes only an obligation to transfer the right of ownership (therefore, it is referred to as an obligational contract or obligational effects of a contract) and the transfer of the right of ownership only takes place upon accession of another fact, e.g., registration in a public register (means of acquisition, *modus acquirendi*), or the transfer of the right of ownership takes place upon the very effectiveness of the transfer contract; in that case, an obligational contract is at the same time a real agreement (we talk about a translational effect of the contract because the right of ownership is transferred by the contract itself).[157]

230. In both cases, however, a transfer contract must be valid and effective, otherwise the right of ownership will not be transferred (transfer of a right of ownership is causal in Czech law, that is, it cannot take place without a valid and effective obligational contract). Where a legal title becomes subsequently invalid (e.g., if its voidability is invoked) or is cancelled (e.g., by withdrawal from a contract), it also has an immediate effect on the right of ownership transferred between the parties. The right of ownership of other acquirers is, however, not extinguished with regard to the principle of legal certainty and protection of acquired rights.[158]

First of all, an obligational contract must define the property being transferred in a sufficiently clear manner, otherwise the contract will not be made at all (section 553(1) of the CC). Immovable property should, therefore, be individualised by stating the municipality, plot number and cadastral area in which the real property is located.[159] On the contrary, the acreage is not a mandatory information for a sufficient individualisation of real property.[160]

§3. Specific Rules for the Transfer of a Right of Ownership

I. Transfer of a Right of Ownership in Property Not Subject to Registration in Public Registers

231. Property not subject to registration in a public register may be movable as well as immovable property.

The consensual principle applies to the transfer of the right of ownership in such property[161] – the right of ownership is transferred *solo consensu*, i.e., upon the transfer contract becoming effective. In this case, the contract itself has transfer (translational) consequences.

232. If movable property is being transferred, the transfer contract may be entered into in any form; in the case of transfer of immovable property, however,

157. A real agreement is a contract for the transfer of ownership not requiring any other formalities; with regard to the division of rights in rem and an obligational right, it differs from an obligational contract, which only establishes an obligation to transfer the ownership – Wilhelm Felgentraeger, *Friedrich Carl v. Savignys Einfluß auf die Übereignungslehre* (Leipzig: Deichertsche Verlagsbuchhandlung Dr Werner Scholl, 1927), 26.
158. *See* Constitutional Court Case No. Pl. ÚS 78/06.
159. Supreme Court Case No. 22 Cdo 1236/2001.
160. Supreme Court Case No. 30 Cdo 2552/2006.
161. Jiří Švestka, Jiří Spáčil, Marta Škárová & Milan Hulmák. *Občanský zákoník. Komentář* (Prague: C. H. Beck, 2009), 765. While CC 1964 was in effect, there was a principle of tradition, that is, a valid and effective handover of the property (tradition) was required in addition to a valid and effective obligational contract for the transfer of a right of ownership, and it was still possible for the parties to agree that the ownership will pass by a mere contract. The principle of tradition applied in this form until 31 Dec. 2013.

the law requires written form (section 560 of the CC) with signatures of the parties on the same instrument (section 561(2) of the CC).

233. The CC allows parties to stipulate a different moment of transfer of a right of ownership than the moment of the contract becoming effective (e.g., handover of the property or payment of the purchase price).

234. The consensual principle of transfer of a right of ownership brings certain problematic moments, especially a risk that third parties may be harmed due to the lack of publicity of the right of ownership (the person who does have property in his possession is no longer its owner). For that reason, the law includes, among other things, a rule for a multiple (repeated) transfer of a right of ownership. In the case of multiple transfers, the right of ownership may be acquired by the person to whom the property is surrendered (section 1100(1) of the CC). The law does not stipulate any requirement of goodwill of the person to whom the property was surrendered. If property is surrendered to a person who was the first person to enter into a contract with the transferor and if that person knows that the transferor subsequently transferred the property again, such a fact will not be to the detriment of that person because the first acquirer became the owner upon the first contract becoming effective. Good faith as a prerequisite of acquisition is, however, significant if property is handed over to a person who entered into a contract later.

II. Transfer of a Right of Ownership in Property Subject to Registration in Public Registers

235. Property subject to registration in a public register may be movable property (e.g., a vessel or a trademark) as well as immovable property (a tract of land or a right of superficies).

The *intabulation principle* applies to the transfer of a right of ownership in such property – a right of ownership is only transferred upon registration in a public register (section 1105 of the CC), i.e., intabulation under a valid and effective obligational contract. Therefore, if registration is made, for example, under an invalid contract, the right of ownership will not be transferred upon the registration of the right of ownership; however, if third parties are in good faith, they may – subject to (other) conditions stipulated in section 984 of the CC, which provides for material publicity of public registers – acquire a right of ownership from a non-entitled person (registered in the books) unless the original owner defends himself using a note on the disputability pursuant to sections 985 and 986 of the CC.

236. An obligational contract on the transfer of real property must be concluded before an application to enter the right of ownership under that contract is filed with the Land Register Office.[162]

162. Supreme Court, Case No. 30 Cdo 4817/2008.

237. A right of ownership in property that has to be registered in the Land Register is registered upon entry in the Land Register, which has constitutive effects (section 6 in combination with section 11(1)(a) of the LRA (Land Register Act)). A registration in the Land Register becomes effective on the date of application for an entry in the Land Register with the relevant Land Register Office; therefore, it has *ex tunc* effects.

238. The intabulation principle does not allow an immediate acquisition of ownership upon conclusion of a contract because a certain period of time will usually pass between its conclusion and registration in a public register, but its advantage is the unity of the moment of acquisition of the right of ownership and its effects vis-à-vis third parties.

239. The intabulation principle of transfer of a right of ownership in immovable property registered in a public register is stipulated as mandatory, that is, it is not possible to agree on a different moment of transfer of the right of ownership than upon the moment of registration in a public register.

240. In the case of transfer of movable property subject to registration in public registers, the transfer contract may be concluded in any form unless the law envisages a special rule; in the case of transfer of immovable property; however, the law requires written form (section 560 of the CC) with signatures of the parties on the same instrument (section 561(2) of the CC).

241. Where a right of ownership is being transferred with respect to property subject to registration in public registers, there may be a situation where the transferor transfers the right to several persons. In these cases, the right of ownership will be acquired by the person whose right of ownership was registered in a public register as first (section 1100(2) of the CC), regardless of the date when he concluded the transfer contract (i.e., in the case of immovable property subject to registration in the Land Register the person who was the first to apply for an entry in the Land Register). It is, however, expressly stated that such a person must be in good faith.

III. Transfer of a Right of Ownership in Generically Defined Property

242. Property defined generically is property that may be replaced by property of the same kind.

A right of ownership in property defined generically may not be transferred before such property is distinguished from other property of the same kind as the subject of a transfer may only be an individually determined item.[163] The moment of transfer, therefore, must not precede the moment of distinction of generically defined property. However, as soon as property is distinguished from other property of the same kind, it becomes subject to rules on the transfer of ownership (i.e., in general, the consensual principle).

163. Eva Dobrovolná in Jiří Spáčil et al., *Občanský zákoník*, 340.

243. If the parties fail to agree on how the property defined will generically be distinguished, specific items will be selected usually by a unilateral act of the transferor. This also corresponds to section 1926(1) of the CC; the seller who is obliged to supply an item may choose the manner of performance. Generically defined items may be distinguished, for example, by their separation from other items, packing or labelling.

IV. Specific Rules for the Transfer of a Right of Ownership

244. Legal orders usually apply the consensual principle for practical reasons and with regard to certain specifics contain a special rule (exception) for the sale of goods in a shop. This is similar in Czech law. In the case of non-self-service sale of goods in a shop, the right of ownership is transferred upon handover of the item (cf. section 2160(1) of the CC). In the case of self-service sale in a shop, the right of ownership is transferred upon payment of the purchase price (section 2160(2) of the CC).

Chapter 2. Transfer of Property by Death

§1. The Broader Context

245. In the Czech legal system, law of inheritance is still understood mostly in the formal legal (objective) sense as a set of norms regulating what happens to a decedent's estate (i.e., its succession to legal successors) and the rights and obligations of a broad range of persons (the decedent, inheritors, legatees, creditors, etc.). In a subjective sense, law of inheritance is understood to be the right of a particular individual to the estate of a deceased natural person or to a proportionate share of such an estate (cf. section 145 of the CC).

However, a certain shift has occurred since the recodification of private law in 2014. Inheritance law is conceived in a broader sense, i.e., not just as inheritance law that is 'provided in statutes' but also as it is established – within the legal limits – through the decedent's will. The broader conception is common in current international legal scholarship not only in neighbouring Germany (Dutta) and Austria (Schuauer et al.) but also in other international contexts (Röthel, Braun, Will Substitutes).

246. The new Czech law of inheritance substantially emphasises the principle of the autonomy of one's will, primarily in the form of so-called testamentary freedom, i.e., the freedom to regulate matters related to one's death by means of one's own demonstration of will. At the same time, some other alternative instruments may be used to 'transfer' property from one generation to another. In some respects, such instruments complement the law of inheritance; in other respects, they actually compete with it.

247. The fundamental feature of hereditary succession is the division of property which may not always be a good thing for property owners (e.g., in cases of succession to 'family' business or to real estate). Such owners may, by contrast, be interested in preserving the unity of the estate. Many are also aware of the risk of deterioration of family relations as a result of the settlement and division of the decedent's estate among the beneficiaries. Problems may also arise where inheritance law affects the rights of persons doing business together with the decedent[164] and who may be interested in continuing their activities, including the preservation of jobs and other related effects.[165]

248. Another reason for seeking out alternative ways of handling hereditary succession consists in the attempt to avoid prolonged and often complicated inheritance proceedings (mainly in order to eliminate the period of uncertainty during the proceedings).[166] Legal practice has also shown that there is some fear from possible

164. This issue is subject to a debate also in Austria; for more details, *see* Susanne Kalss in Astrid Deixler-Hübner & Martin Schauer, *Erbrecht* NEU (Wien: Lexis Nexis, 2015), 95 et seq.
165. *Ibid.*
166. Alexandra Braun & Anne Röthel, *Passing Wealth on Death: Will-Substitutes in Comparative Perspective* (Oxford and Portland, Oregon: Hart Publishing, 2016), 341 et seq.

claims raised after the death of the testator by creditors[167] and other third persons. Last but not least, there are also tax reasons (and related fees and costs) that play a significant (and often decisive) role when choosing the most suitable way of passing property from one generation to another.[168]

249. Because of that, people seeking to make hereditary dispositions frequently avail themselves of not only the possibility of making a testamentary gift (*donatio mortis causa*) but also of establishing a foundation (either a foundation or an endowment fund), a trust or some other trust-like form (a trust fund in the Czech legal system), or setting up a business corporation for the purpose of administering the property. In the broadest sense of the word, this category also includes such instruments as life insurance policies specifying particular beneficiaries, since such insurance – from a functional point of view – is likewise a kind of 'disposition in the event of death' that essentially excludes testamentary succession.

250. In other countries (both European and non-European), similar concepts and institutes may be found, often under the same names but with a somewhat different content. The term that has come to be used in other countries for this relatively open set of instruments for the trans-generational transfer of property is '*will substitutes*'. This phenomenon has been subject to an increasing attention over the past decade or so.[169]

251. The application of such instruments in practice gives rise to many complex issues because law of inheritance has frequently survived in many European countries in its original form since the times of the major codifications. It often conflicts with the above-mentioned alternative instruments, particularly as far as the position and rights of forced heirs are concerned. All of that gives rise to tensions whenever some international elements are at stake (e.g., in the case of trusts established under foreign laws) – a situation that is not that unusual due to the current processes of Europeanisation and globalisation.

§2. An Outline of Inheritance Law under the CC

252. The characteristic feature of current Czech inheritance law is its respect for the will of the deceased person and the heirs. That marks a major departure from the legal regulation valid until the end of 2013 and a return to the traditional conception adhered to across Europe, which was likewise valid in this country until 1950.

167. This issue is currently being debated in the Czech Republic in connection with the change of the extent of heirs' duty to settle the deceased person's debts.
168. In the Czech legal system, the tax burden of hereditary succession is not as acute as in some other countries (such as the UK, where the basic rate of inheritance tax amounts to 40%).
169. Martin Schauer in Francesco Schurr, *Handbuch des Vermögensschutzes* (Wien: Manz, 2015).

253. So-called testamentary freedom (i.e., the freedom to dispose of one's own property after one's death) is understood, with respect to the decedent, as a derivative of the freedom of ownership. On the part of the heirs, the autonomy of will is manifested in their possibility to accept, refuse, renounce or alienate the inheritance.

254. In private law (law of inheritance), the principle of the autonomy of will is somewhat in conflict with the familiarity principle (family solidarity). The principle concerns the interest to preserve the property 'within a family', i.e., it is based on the presumption that the decedent's estate should pass on to the deceased's person's blood relations in the spirit of preserving family solidarity. It is manifested mainly in the protection of forced heirs. While this conception is typical of continental Europe (unlike determining rules in the Anglo-American system), it has been gradually redefined (namely weakened) over the past few decades in connection with the changing perception of the position and function of the family (the weakening of family links and the conception of social welfare), mainly in view of enhancing the autonomy of the decedent's will.

255. The new Czech CC has brought about a major change in the conception of the rights of forced heirs by substantially weakening their position. Not only did the recodification reduce the amount of the compulsory share but it also gives such heirs 'nothing more' than the right to have the value of their compulsory share matched in money (section 1654(1) of the CC). In this sense, the CC essentially represents a return to the tradition of the Austrian ABGB. At the same time, however, it apparently has not abandoned the 'narrow' conception of the defence of forced heirs contained in CC 1964 as a mechanism that seeks nothing more than to moderate the manner in which the value of the decedent's estate is to be distributed, and not to interfere with any other property dispositions by the decedent.

256. Another typical feature of Czech inheritance law is the assistance of the state during the acquisition/settlement of the inheritance, which is meant to contribute to the meeting of the decedent's will and to the protection of the rights of all persons involved in the property settlement, including creditors' protection.

257. Inheritance law is 'activated' upon the testator's death (section 1479 of the CC), which constitutes the starting point of hereditary succession. Inheritance is acquired with effect as of the date of the decedent's death. The judicial decision confirming the acquisition of property in inheritance proceedings, which is started by operation of law, has a merely declaratory character (it merely declares the existence of a right). However, since the related procedural regulation has significant imperfections, the testator is frequently motivated to look for alternative instruments, as specified above.

258. A competent heir is a person who lives until the descent of hereditary succession and who enjoys the hereditary title. An heir may inherit property unless there is some reason resulting in his or her unworthiness to inherit (sections 1481–1483 of the CC); or unless the heir renounces the inheritance on the basis of a prior agreement with the decedent; or unless the heir is lawfully disinherited or refuses or renounces the right to inherit. At the same time, the heir must enjoy the hereditary title.

259. All of the decedent's assets (property and claims) and liabilities (debts) pass onto the heir. While this construction strengthens the protection of the creditors, it gives the heir the right to delimit the extent of his or her obligation to settle the testator's debts by means of issuing a so-called reservation of the list of estate. Where the heir seeks the reservation of the list of estate, he or she is liable for the decedent's debts only within the limit of the amount of inheritance acquired.

260. In section 1491, the CC provides that dispositions *mortis causa* are *inheritance agreement, testament and codicil.* Some of those dispositions may likewise contain the decedent's demonstration of will to establish a legacy, a foundation or an endowment fund, or a trust fund. It is also possible to conclude an inheritance gift contract (*donatio mortis causa*).

261. A disposition *mortis causa* may not reduce the compulsory share of forced heirs who have not refused their right to the compulsory share or been disinherited. Where the disposition *mortis caus*a is in conflict, any forced heir is entitled to a compulsory share (section 1492 of the CC). However, where forced heirs are overlooked, the disposition *mortis causa* is not automatically rendered void; rather, it entitles the heir to a monetary payment equal to the amount of his or her compulsory share.

262. An *inheritance agreement* is the 'strongest' (and preferred) inheritance title.[170] Thus, it has a priority over testamentary and statutory succession. It constitutes a bilateral legal act whereby the decedent appoints the other party or some third party as the heir (or the legatee) and the beneficiary accepts that role. However, the decedent may freely dispose of his or her property while still alive: the beneficiary is entitled only to what is left of the inheritance after the decedent's death.

263. The law places a special requirement on formal aspects, requiring the form of a public deed (a notarial deed) and personal acts (it is not possible to be represented). An inheritance agreement may not dispose of the entire decedent's estate (one-quarter must remain 'available' for other dispositions, e.g., a testament). The inheritance agreement may be cancelled upon the consent of both parties. If the decedent prepares or concludes a gift agreement *mortis causa* and if such an agreement is not compatible with the inheritance agreement, then the contractual heir may seek such legal acts to be declared as void. The law provides a specific regime for the regulation of spouses who conclude an inheritance agreement. Since a

170. Roman Fiala & Ljubomír Drápal et al., *Občanský zákoník IV. Dědické právo (§ 1475-1720). Komentář* (Prague: C. H. Beck, 2015), 280.

divorce does not automatically cancel the effects of an inheritance agreement, it is advisable for the agreement to provide an explicit specification of the legal relations in case of a divorce.

264. *A testament* (section 1494 of the CC) is a unilateral, unaddressed, personal and revocable demonstration of the decedent's will for the event of his or her death, whereby the decedent disposes of his or her property (or a share thereof) or a legacy to one or more persons. The testament must be executed in person; no representation is possible. The testator may make a testament about the whole or any part of his or her estate. The remaining part of the estate will be subject to statutory succession (unless an inheritance agreement has been concluded or a legacy declared). Testamentary succession has a priority over statutory (intestate) succession.

265. In general, the law requires that a testament should be in writing. Different requirements are placed to an allographic testament (written on a computer, for instance, and signed in one's own hand in the presence of two witnesses), a holographic testament (written in one's own handwriting), and a testament in the form of a public deed (a notarial deed). Where the testament has the form of a public deed, the notary public is obliged to preserve the information and enter it in the Record of Legal Acts for the Event of Death, maintained by the Notarial Chamber of the Czech Republic.

266. Special requirements are placed on illiterate persons unable to read or write and on persons with a limited legal capacity. Minors over the age of 15 may make a testament in the form of a public deed (without the consent of a legal representative. A special case is the so-called privileged testament (sections 1542 et seq. of the CC) made during an unexpected event under an evident and immediate threat to the decedent's life or under exceptional circumstances (e.g., during natural disasters, wars). However, such a testament loses its validity after the passage of a certain period of time after the removal of such unexpected circumstances.

267. The content of a testament must be formulated in a clear and certain manner. There is a special interpretative rule stipulating that the decedent's will should be followed as closely as possible (section 1494(2) of the CC). The essential elements of a testament include the testator's own signature and a designation of the heir. In addition, the testator may include a supplementary annex containing the conditions, stipulating the time and laying out the instructions that oblige the future heirs or limit their rights. However, the law places some limits on the testator in this respect (against arbitrariness, violation of public order, etc.). The appointment of an executor of a will or an administrator of property is sometimes considered to constitute the content of such a supplementary annex.

268. The testator may revoke the testament or any of its provisions at any time. The testament is revoked by means of a revocation or the making of a later testament. The making of a later testament revokes the earlier testament in the extent to which the earlier testament does not compare with the later one.

269. In a *codicil*, the testator may order that a legacy be handed down, stipulate that the heir or legatee be subject to a condition, or stipulate time, or impose an order upon a legatee or an heir. A codicil does not constitute an inheritance title because it does not appoint heirs. There is a difference between a testamentary codicil (made in addition to a testament) and an intestate codicil (made without a testament).

270. By *establishing a legacy*, a claim (to be filled by the heir) is being created for a legatee to be given a certain thing, or a thing or several things of a certain kind, or for a certain right to be established. Upon the decedent's death, the legatee acquires the right to the legacy for himself or herself and his or her successors. Since he or she is not an heir, the legatee is not obliged to cover the decedent's debts.

The decedent establishes a legacy by ordering a certain person, in a disposition *mortis causa* (i.e., a testament, an inheritance agreement or a codicil), to surrender the subject matter of the legacy to the legatee. A legacy may be established only by a person with the legal capacity to make a will. A legatee may only be a person with the legal capacity to inherit. Legacies are a burden to all the heirs according to their shares even where a thing that is subject to the legacy belongs to only one of the co-heirs.

271. *Forced heirs* are the decedent's children. Where the children do not inherit, then the forced heirs are their descendants. Forced heirs are entitled to a compulsory share of the decedent's estate. Where a forced heir is a minor, he or she must receive at least three-quarters of his or her statutory inheritance share. Where a forced heir is an adult, he or she must receive at least one-quarter of his or her statutory inheritance share.

272. A forced heir may be validly disinherited. Disinheritance is the decedent's unilateral legal act whereby he or she excludes a forced heir from his or her right to a compulsory share. The law provides an explicit enumeration of reasons for disinheritance (section 1646 of the CC). Thus, *disinheritance* is possible where the forced heir:

- has failed to provide necessary help to the decedent when needed;
- does not show true interest in the decedent, contrary to expectations;
- has been sentenced for a criminal offence committed under circumstances attesting to his or her perverse nature; or
- constantly lives an unrestrained life.

Although the reason for inheritance does not have to be expressly stated in the disinheritance declaration, it must be subsequently proved. The disinheritance declaration may be made or changed or revoked in the same manner in which a testament is made or revoked.

273. The compulsory share may be established in the form of an inheritance share or legacy but it may not be encumbered in any way to the forced heir. The possibility of receiving an advance of one's compulsory share (so-called *collation*) is a demonstration of the effort to keep a certain proportionality of property performance for the benefit of forced heirs. The advance on one's share does not constitute a usual donation. Any instructions by the decedent limiting the compulsory share are disregarded.

274. Where there is no heir in the inheritance agreement or testament and the decedent fails to specify his or her will through some other statutory instrument, there is *succession at law – statutory intestate succession.* The law provides six groups of heirs that are subject to representation[171] and accretion.[172]

275. The first group of heirs consists of the decedent's children and spouse (or partner, cf. section 3020 of the CC), with each inheriting an equal share. Where some child does not inherit, his or her share is equally acquired by his or her children; the same holds for more distant descendants of the same ancestor (representation). The spouse cannot inherit the property exclusively in the first group.

276. Where the decedent's descendants do not inherit, then comes the second group that consists of the spouse (or partner), the decedent's parents and other persons who lived in the same household with the decedent for a period of least one year prior to the decedent's death while taking care of the common household or being dependent for maintenance on the decedent (so-called cohabiting persons).

277. The heirs in the second group inherit an equal share, with the spouse always receiving at least one-half of the estate. Where none of the decedent's parents or a cohabiting person inherits, then the spouse is entitled to the entire estate. Where at least one of the persons specified above inherits, then the decedent's spouse is entitled to one-half of the property. The father, the mother and the cohabiting person inherit the second half of the estate, with each inheriting an equal share. A freed share of any of those persons results in the increase of the other heirs' shares within the relevant half of the estate (accretion). A cohabiting person may not be the only heir in the second group. Where no spouse or none of the parents inherit, then the third group of heirs is applicable. The third group consists of the decedent's siblings and cohabiting persons. Where some of the decedent's siblings do not inherit, then his or her inheritance share is acquired in an equal amount by his or her children (representation of the decedent's nephews and nieces). If there is no heir in the third group, then the fourth group of heirs is applicable, with the decedent's grandparents inheriting an equal amount. Where none of the heirs in the fourth group inherit, then the fifth group of heirs is applicable, with the decedent's great grandparents inheriting. The grandparents of the decedent's father inherit one-half of the estate and the grandparents of the decedent's mother inherit the other half of the estate. Both groups of grandparents inherit an equal share of the relevant half. Where a particular member of the pair does not inherit, then the freed share of one-eighth is inherited by the second member (accretion of a freed inheritance share). Where the pair

171. Representation means that the heir's successors step into a freed inheritance share.
172. Accretion means that the freed inheritance share increases to the other heirs from the same group of heirs.

does not inherit, then their quarter is inherited by the other pair of the same side. Where none of the pairs of a given side inherits, then the estate passes to the pairs of the other side in the same proportion in which they share the half of the estate that is inherited by them directly. Where none of the heirs in the fifth group inherits, then the sixth group of heirs is applicable, with the children of the decedent's siblings' children and the children of the decedent's grandparents inheriting an equal share. Where some of the children of the decedent's grandparents do not inherit, then his or her children (i.e., uncles and aunts or also nephews and nieces due to the application of representation) inherit.

278. In addition, the CC establishes a *special right of some persons for maintenance*, which comes in the form of a statutory legacy having a social meaning. It delimits a group of persons (a forced heir without the right to a compulsory share, a surviving spouse, a pregnant widow, a mother of the decedent's child, a surviving parent, a cohabiting person) who are given the right to maintenance within the (limited) extent provided by law. This right may be asserted with the heir, given the conditions stipulated in advance.

279. Where there is no heir, the estate passes to the state ('*escheat*'). The state is then considered as if it was a statutory heir. However, the state does not have the right to refuse the inheritance. Also, the role of the state is in some other respects different.

280. Where the person identified as the heir does not acquire the inheritance, the law of inheritance gives the right to that person to appoint a substitute. This situation is called '*general substitution*'.

281. The testator may order that, upon the death of an heir (or upon the meeting of some other condition), the property passes to a *fideicommissary* as a subsequent heir. The heir shall assume the inheritance but, after the condition specified by the decedent is met, the inheritance passes to the subsequent heir. This fideicommissary substitution has a temporal limitation and terminates no later than after the passage of one hundred years after the death of the testator, even if it has been established for a longer period of time. Where a thing and its owner are entered into a public list, fideicommissum is registered in such a list as well.

282. The possibility of *disposing of one's inheritance* is a demonstration of the autonomy of will on the side of people – heirs – acceding into the decedent's rights and obligations. An heir may, after the decedent's death, refuse the inheritance, being able to do so typically no later than one month after the heir is notified by the court of his or her right to refuse to inherit and of the consequences of such an action. A *refusal of inheritance* is required to be an express declaration to the court. A contractual heir may refuse the inheritance only where the inheritance agreement does not exclude that possibility. If the inheritance is refused by a forced heir, he or she can refuse it except for the compulsory share. Where an heir refuses to inherit, he or she is considered as if he or she has never acquired the inheritance.

283. An heir who has not turned down inheritance may *renounce* it during probate proceedings in court for the benefit of some other heir; in such a case, the forced heir also renounces his or her right to a compulsory share, with effect for his or her descendants too.

284. An heir may likewise *alienate the inheritance* after the death of the decedent by means of an agreement in the form of a public deed. Upon such an alienation, the legal assignee assumes the rights and obligations vested in the inheritance. Because of protection of third party rights, the law provides that the legal assignee and the alienator of the inheritance are jointly and severally liable for any decedent's debts.

285. A special case occurs when the inheritance is *relinquished* (by means of a contract during the decedent's life), although it concerns the legal action of an assumed heir. Such a demonstration of will may be relevant for the further arrangement of the decedent *mortis causa*, as well as for other (co-)heirs.

§3. Procedural Issues: A Diversion

286. Inheritance proceedings are regulated in Chapter III of the Special Judicial Proceedings (SJP). During the proceedings, the notary public acts in the role of a judicial commissioner and makes judicial acts. The court confirms inheritance to those who have not refused the inheritance and who enjoy, given the course of the proceedings, the best inheritance title. The court will confirm to a single heir the fact that he or she has acquired the inheritance. The court will state who the heir is, whose inheritance is being acquired, for what reason and whether the heir acquires it with or without making a reservation or an inventory. In the case of several heirs, the court will confirm their inheritance shares in the amounts offsetting any possible advances on inheritance share and offsetting any legacies. When dividing the estate, the court will also confirm what inheritance is being acquired by each of the heirs and what the reason is for dividing the estate. During the court inheritance proceedings, the heirs may agree on the amounts of their inheritance shares. The court approves the agreement as long as it is not in conflict with the interests of a person under special protection (i.e., a natural person without a full legal capacity or a person who is not known or present, or a publicly beneficial legal person or a legal person established in a public interest). Where heirs inherit on the basis of testamentary dispositions *mortis causa*, they may agree on different amounts of their inheritance shares than those determined by the testator only as long as the testator has expressly provided for that possibility.

Chapter 3. Possession

§1. Definition of Possession

I. Introduction

287. Czech legislation classifies possession as a right in rem. This is relatively questionable in legal theory; many authors consider possession rather as a factual state protected by law.[173]

Possession can be defined as factual control over tangible property (*corpus possessionis*) with the intention of having it for oneself (*animus possidendi*). The Czech CC considers only rights (not things) as the subject of possession, specifically property rights that are transferable and allow permanent or repeated exercise.[174] The subject of possession may not only be especially a right of ownership but also other rights – e.g., a servitude or obligational rights. In this sense, the law also distinguishes between possession of a right of ownership and possession of other rights.

288. Possession as a factual state should be distinguished from the right itself (e.g., a right of ownership). While the possessor is a person who controls the property by being in control of it and has the intention to have it for himself, the owner is a person who as an absolute right in rem in that property and to whom the property belongs (however, the owner need not be in control of the property and need not factually control it). Therefore, the owner and the possessor may be either the same person or different persons.[175]

289. Furthermore, in the case of immovable property, where a person is registered as the owner in the Land Register, this does not necessarily mean that he is also the possessor if he does not effectively exercise that right. If someone is registered in public books as a landowner but does not effectively control the land, he has a 'book possession'. A mere book possession, therefore, is not an actual possession.[176] Therefore, if a certain person does not effectively, i.e., through his own power, control the property (cf. below under II), he cannot exercise possession.[177] Simply put – a person who is registered as an owner in the Land Register although he is not one in fact and who does not effectively exercise possession with respect to the tract of land may not acquire a right of ownership by long-term possession (by acquisitive prescription – cf. below Chapter 3, §2).

173. Jiří Spáčil in Jiří Spáčil et al., *Občanský zákoník*, 66 et seq.
174. Section 988(1) of the CC.
175. Let us give the following example: A starts using part of B's tract of land in the belief that the tract of land is his, that is, that it belongs to A. These may be cases where a buyer buys real property e.g., under a void contract (e.g., due to lack of legal capacity on the part of the transferor) and seizes possession, or buys real property but starts using also part of an adjacent land due to 'addition by fencing'. While B is the owner of the entire tract of land in the first case and of the part of the tract of land in the second case, A is its possessor.
176. Supreme Court Case No. Rv I 75/31.
177. Supreme Court Case No. 22 Cdo 3894/2017.

290. Possession has several effects in the Czech legal order. First, it may lead (under conditions provided for by law) to original acquisition of a right of ownership by acquisitive prescription. Moreover, it is an indication of a right of ownership. This applies especially to movable property, where possession gives rise to legal appearance that the person who possesses certain property is its owner (it fulfils the function of publicity). This is then taken into account in the provision on the acquisition from a non-entitled person (cf. Part I, Chapter 3; Part II, Chapter 3) which allows acquisition of a right of ownership in good faith if a third party relies on the transferor's right of ownership although the transferor was not the owner. Finally, possession is also subject to protection; the legal order protects it (although it is a factual state) in principle in two ways – by self-help and in court proceedings (cf. Part III, Chapter 3, §1, VII).

II. Exercise of a Right and Possession Will

291. A prerequisite of possession is a *factual control over property* or *exercise of the possessed right.* This need not include only physical control (the possessor has the property directly with him in his hand) but also factual handling (he has the property in his control, e.g., in his apartment). The person who effectively controls a property is a person who exercises, according to general opinions and experience, legal dominion over that property. Therefore, the possessor of a tract of land is also a person who has not actually entered it in a long time unless another person seizes possession, and also a person who exercises possession through another person (referred to as detentor). It is, however, necessary that the detentor physically controls the property for the possessor on the possessor's behalf, e.g., as his lessee.[178]

292. However, if a situation is to be classified as possession, the exercise of the right must be accompanied by the *intention to have the property for oneself*, and such will must be obvious externally (it is not sufficient if the possessor only thinks that and does not express his will in any apparent way). If the will to exercise the right for oneself lacks, the situation is not classified as possession. Such a situation is referred to as detention. A detentor, therefore, is a person who only effectively controls certain property. This may include, for example, a lessee, a pledgee or a depositary. Detention does not have the same position in the legal order as possession; however, law protects legitimate detention against unauthorised interference.[179]

178. Supreme Court Case No. 22 Cdo 728/2000.
179. An entitled detentor is, similarly to an owner, granted the right to protection against unauthorised interference by other persons. A detentor may thus request rendition of property or its clearance by means of an action for recovery (*reivindicatio*) and also refrainment from other interference by means of an *actio negatoria* – cf. s. 1044 of the CC.

III. The Person of the Possessor

293. Possessors may be legal entities as well as natural persons, and possession by several persons (co-possession) is allowed – in such a case, property could be acquired, subject to fulfilment of statutory conditions, into co-ownership or, in the case of spouses, into community property;[180] however, provided that the prerequisites of acquisitive prescription have been met (especially good faith) in all co-owners. Otherwise, a right of ownership may not be acquired by prescription, including into the exclusive ownership of one of the co-owners.[181]

IV. Kinds of Possession

294. The CC defines three kinds of possession – lawful, genuine and in good faith. Their distinction is particularly important in assessing the conditions of acquisitive prescription. Not every possession leads to acquisitive prescription (cf. Part III, Chapter 3, §2). Distinguishing between kinds of possession also plays a role, for example, in assessing claims of a possessor in good faith and a possessor in bad faith.[182]

295. Lawful possession is possession based on a valid legal cause.[183] This includes, in particular, a contract eligible for acquisition of a right (e.g., a contract of sale or donation), and such a contract must be valid. Where a contract is invalid, possession is not lawful. The very fact that a party was not entitled to dispose of the subject of performance under the contract at the time the contract was concluded does not in itself invalidate the contract (section 1760 of the CC). This means that if someone acquires property from a transferor under an (otherwise) valid contract, he acquires lawful possession although the transferor was not the owner. A lawful transferor is not a person who only believes that he has a valid legal cause.[184]

296. Possession in good faith is possession where the possessor has a convincing reason to believe that he has the right he exercises. Good faith must be based on an excusable misconception about the existence of the possessed right. On the contrary, a person who knows or to whom it must be evident from the circumstances that the right he exercises does not pertain to him is a possessor in bad faith.[185]

297. Genuine possession is possession acquired wilfully, in secret or by trickery, or possession by a person seeking to transform into a permanent right what

180. The Czech CC establishes a statutory property regime of spouses, which is created already upon marriage. This is a kind of estate by entirety – cf. ss 708 et seq. of the CC.
181. Jiří Švestka, Jiří Spáčil & Milan Hulmák et al., *Občanský zákoník. Komentář. Volume 1* (Prague: C. H. Beck, 2009), 813.
182. Section 996 of the CC.
183. Jiří Spáčil in Jiří Švestka, Jiří Spáčil & Milan Hulmák et al., *Občanský zákoník. Komentář. Volume 1* (Prague: C. H. Beck, 2009), 773.
184. Jiří Spáčil in Jiří Spáčil, *Věcná práva*, 35.
185. Section 992(1) of the CC.

belonged to him only in the form of a precarious loan. An example of a wilful acquisition of possession is the theft of property. Possession is acquired by trickery if a person acquires possession by an acquisition act which he conceals from the current possessor. The latter concerns situations where someone is allowed (by means of precarious loan) to walk through a tract of land, the precarious loan terminates and he continues to walk through that tract of land (he is thus a non-genuine holder of the right – in this case of a servitude of a right of way).

V. Claims of a Possessor in Good Faith and in Bad Faith

298. A *possessor in good faith* may, within the limits stipulated by law, possess, use, destroy or otherwise dispose of property. The law is based on the assumption that the possessor is not liable to anyone for that.[186] A possessor in good faith is also entitled to revenues and fruits of the property. It also follows from the above that the possessor is not obliged to reimburse the property owner for unjust enrichment in the amount of the due rent for the period of possession in good faith. A possessor in good faith is reimbursed by the possessor for the necessary costs required to continuously preserve the essence of property, as well as the reasonably incurred costs which increase the usefulness or the value of the property. A possessor in good faith may not, however, claim reimbursement of usual maintenance costs (these are to be paid by the possessor due to the fact that he was using the property at the time of his possession in good faith and, where applicable, had revenues from it).

299. If a possessor in good faith incurred costs on the property as a result of a hobby or for decoration, only the amount of increase of the usual value of the property is to be paid. Before surrendering the property, the possessor may remove such adjustments and keep what has been attached to the property in this way and what can be separated without deteriorating the essence of the property.[187]

300. A *possessor in bad faith*, on the contrary, is obliged to surrender to the owner all the revenues and damage that arose from his possession. He is only entitled to reimbursement of costs necessary to preserve the property.[188]

VI. Acquisition of Possession

301. In principle, possession can be acquired in two ways, *directly and derivatively*. Possession is acquired directly by one's own power, i.e., its extent is determined by the possessor (e.g., appropriation). Possession is acquired derivatively to the extent possessed by the current possessor who transfers the possession to his legal successor (e.g., in contractual acquisition or inheritance). In the case of derivative acquisition, handover and takeover of property (tradition) take place; Czech law

186. Section 996 of the CC.
187. Jiří Spáčil in Jiří Spáčil, *Věcná práva*, 37.
188. Sections 1000 and 1001 of the CC.

also allows a symbolic tradition (e.g., handover of keys from real property) as well as *constitutum possesorium* (the property remains which the transferor who possesses it for the transferee) or *traditio brevi manu* (the property is acquired by its detentor, e.g., a lessee, so a physical handover of the property does not take place).

VII. Extinction of Possession

302. Possession is extinguished if waived by the possessor or if the possessor becomes permanently unable to exercise the content of the right which he has so far been exercising. The former case concerns, for example, handover of property to another person or abandonment of tangible property. The latter case does not concern a mere failure to use property but, for example, permanent loss of property.

VIII. Protection of Possession

303. Legal regulation of protection of possession is based on the assumption that no one is entitled to disturb the possession of another.[189] The purpose of protection of possession is to provide a quick and informal protection of the last possession of the possessor against a wilful interference in his possession.[190]

304. Possession may primarily be protected by *self-help* under the conditions stipulated in section 14 of the CC. Where conditions of admissible self-help are not met, the possessor must file an action seeking protection of possession before the court.

Protection is enjoyed by the last possession but need not necessarily be peaceful, i.e., last for a certain time in the sense of non-existence of previous interference with the possession.[191]

305. Therefore, the quality of possession is not taken into account in the proceedings, and unlawful possession, non-genuine possession and possession in bad faith also enjoy protection. The purpose of such regulation is to prevent wilfulness, which is prohibited in the rule of law.

It is also necessary to distinguish between *protection of a right* (e.g., a right of ownership) that establishes a right of possession for the entitled person (and therefore also petitory protection – *petitorium*) and *protection of possession* that provides protection of the last possession against wilful interference. *Petitory actions*

189. Jiří Spáčil, *Ochrana vlastnictví a držby v občanském zákoníku* (Prague: C. H. Beck, 2005), 235.
190. This corresponds not only to the substantive regulation in the CC (ss 1003–1008 of the CC, i.e., a description of what is protected) but also the subsequent procedural regulation (ss 176–180 of the Code of Civil Procedure).
191. Jiří Spáčil in Jiří Spáčil et al., *Občanský zákoník,* 325.

are, in particular, owner's actions (i.e., an action for recovery of property or clearance; *actio negatoria*, which seeks hindering of other interference in the ownership of real estate that its unlawful detention,[192] or an action seeking determination of the right of ownership).

306. When the court is considering an action seeking protection of possession, it must not take into account any result of a petitory dispute.[193]

307. The possessor may seek restoration of the original state and/or refrainment from further interference with the possessor by an action seeking protection of possession. Both requirements correspond to the content of the plea in petitory (owner's) actions (action for recovery of property – in the case of immovable property for clearance – and *actio negatoria*).

308. Protection of possession may not be sought only by a *possessor of a right of ownership* but also by a *possessor of another right.* This way, a lessee who has been wilfully disturbed in this possession of a right of lease, e.g., by the fact that someone removed from him or started using the leased property may seek further exercise of the possession in the form of return of the property or refraining from interference consisting in its unlawful detention.

309. An action seeking protection of possession, however, can be successful only if it has been proven that the possessor had (a) the *last possession* and (b) that there has been a *wilful interference* with or *expulsion from the possession.* Such facts may be subject of evidence taking in a hearing ordered at the discretion of the court.[194]

310. In proceedings in which protection of possession is sought, it is by no means possible to raise objections to the nature of the possession, the right to possess the property, claim damages or other claims. The only applicable objection is an objection of non-genuine possession.[195] Non-genuine possessor may file an action to protect his possession but if he had acquired the possession in a non-genuine manner with respect to the defendant and the defendant objects that, the court will dismiss the possessory action.[196]

---

192. For example, unauthorised trucking of concrete panels to a land.
193. For example, if an action seeking protection of possession is filed by a possessor who has possessed the right of ownership in a garden and his possession had been wilfully disturbed by the defendant (the actual garden owner) in such a way that it has prevented the possessor from exercising the possession e.g., by fencing the tract of land, the court must not take into account the fact that the defendant is the owner of the garden.
194. Section 177(1) of the CPC.
195. Section 1007(1) second sentence of the CC.
196. For example, if person A steals property from person B and person B removes the property (not by self-help) from person A, whereupon person A files a possessory action, person B may object that person A had acquired the possession in a non-genuine manner (wilfully).

§2. Acquisition of the Right of Ownership by Acquisitive Prescription

I. Introduction

311. *Acquisitive prescription* is the most common original method of creation of a right of ownership in practice. Legal practice encounters cases of acquisitive prescription under the legal regulation in effect until 31 December 2013 (before recodification; CC 1964) as well as under the CC. Therefore, the present text will deal with both regulations.

312. To assess which regulation will govern the creation of a right of ownership, the moment of acquisition of the right of ownership by acquisitive prescription is of essence. If the date was before 1 January 2014, the issue of acquisition of ownership will be assessed under the relevant provisions of CC 1964.[197] Therefore, the claims (plea) of the person acquiring his right by prescription will be decisive in this respect.[198]

313. The law stipulates that a right of ownership is acquired by prescription based on a *long-term qualified possession*. The original owner loses his right of ownership by acquisitive prescription and the new owner acquires it without being to compensate anyone. A registration in a public register (in the Land Register with respect to tracts of land) is not necessary for the acquisition of a right of ownership by acquisitive prescription. It is, however, in the interest of the possessor who has acquired a right of ownership by prescription to reconcile the registered and actual state, otherwise there is a risk that a right of ownership in property (in immovable property in the case of the Land Register) will be acquired by another person acting in good faith and relying on the correctness of the entry in that public list (cf. Part I, Chapter 3). Therefore, acquisitive prescription also acts against owners registered in books regardless of what legal fact they derive the right of ownership from and whether they had that right until the passage of the acquisitive prescription period. If the person who possesses the whole property fulfils the conditions for acquisitive prescription, it is irrelevant how the existing owners had acquired the property and in the case they were not possessors, their belief or good faith that they are the owners are insignificant if they do not manifest them vis-à-vis the possessor.[199]

314. Qualified possession and expiry of an acquisitive prescription period is required for the acquisition of ownership by acquisitive prescription (therefore, not every possession leads to acquisition of ownership by acquisitive prescription).

197. Section 3028(1) and (2) of the CC, in case law e.g., Supreme Court Case No. 22 Cdo 1339/2018.
198. This will be of practical importance especially in relation to extraordinary acquisitive prescription, which can be objected since 1 Jan. 2019 (cf. below and s. 3066 of the CC). If a possessor claims that he acquired his right of ownership by prescription after 1 Jan. 2019, lawful possession, i.e., possession based on a valid legal acquisition title, will not be necessary for acquisitive prescription.
199. Supreme Court Case No. 22 Cdo 3202/2018.

Acquisitive prescription reflects the fact that a long-term factual state has to be reconciled with the legal state, for reasons of legal certainty. The purpose of the institution of acquisitive prescription is not to forcibly deprive the original owner of his right of ownership.[200]

II. Acquisitive Prescription Pursuant to CC 1964

A. *Property Eligible for Acquisitive Prescription*

315. For an *acquisitive prescription* to take place, it was primarily required that the property subject to acquisitive prescription be also eligible for acquisitive prescription.[201] In relation to tracts of land, case law of the Supreme Court was relevant; it concluded that even a part of a tract of land is eligible for acquisitive prescription.[202]

316. Although, in general, acquisitive prescription of immovable assets was not admissible under CC 1964 due to a narrow conception of property as a tangible item, legal practice allowed acquisitive prescription of a co-ownership share in property.[203] On the other hand, it was not possible to acquire, e.g., a right of lease or a pre-emptive right to a tract of land by prescription,[204] and this conclusion will probably remain unchanged also in relation to the new regulation in the CC.

B. *Possession*

317. *See* above Part III, Chapter 3, §1.

C. *Acquisitive Prescription Period*

318. Due to the fact that until 31 March 1983 it was not possible to acquire a right of ownership in immovable property by prescription because legislation did not envisage such an institution, it was questionable how to address this after 1 January 1992, when legislation (after an amendment to the CC by Act No. 509/1991 Sb.) allowed acquisitive prescription. The case law of the Supreme Court concluded that acquisitive prescription of a right of ownership by natural persons could only take place from 1 January 1992 and only in the case of persons who at any time after 1 January 1992 meet the statutory conditions; moreover, the acquisitive prescription period also included the time for which the entitled possessor had a tract of land in continuous possession before 1 January 1992.

200. Constitutional Court Case No. ÚS I. ÚS 360/06.
201. Bohuslav Petr, *Nabývání vlastnictví originárním způsobem* (Praha: C. H. Beck, 2011), 61.
202. Supreme Court Case No. R 40/2000.
203. Supreme Court Case No. 22 Cdo 459/2007.
204. Supreme Court Case No. 26 Cdo 2080/98; Supreme Court Case No. 28 Cdo 805/2009.

319. The acquisitive prescription period was three years for movable property and ten years for immovable property (i.e., also tracts of land). In any event, however, the period had to be uninterrupted, i.e., the possessor was required to exercise possession throughout the necessary acquisitive prescription period. On the contrary, the acquisitive prescription period was not affected by any change in the owner or possessor (where the possessor was an entitled possessor).

D. Lawful Possession

320. Eligible for acquisitive prescription was only *lawful possession* (similar to possession in good faith – *see* Part III, Chapter 3, §1, IV); the explanation below can in principle be used by analogy for the assessment of possession in good faith under the CC), that is, possession by a possessor who was, given all the circumstances, in good faith that the property in question belonged to him or that the right be exercised belonged to him (section 130(1) first sentence of the 1964 CC).

321. Even a possessor who seized possession based on a void legal act could be entitled. Essential for qualification of possession as lawful was the fact whether the possessor was, given all circumstances, in good faith that he was the subject of the possessed right, that is, he could not know about the cases for invalidity of the contract even while maintaining the usual degree of caution that can be required from everyone given the circumstances of the specific case.[205]

322. There are often cases in practice where possession lasts for a relatively long period and a question arises subsequently whether the possession is lawful. In this respect, the Supreme Court concludes that long-term possession, especially when it lasts for at least thirty to fifty years, indicates good faith of the possessor; with regard to usual care of property, one can assume the original owner would have undoubtedly proceeded to resolve the issue if he had believed that his land is being used by another person. The case law thus addressed cases that are now subject to extraordinary acquisitive prescription.[206]

323. The law stipulated that in case of doubts, the possession must be presumed lawful (section 130(1) of the 1964 CC). This means that the burden of proof with respect to the fact that possession was not lawful is borne by the original landowner (similar regulation is contained in section 994 of the CC).

324. In assessing good faith, one always must take into account whether the possessor had or could have, with usual (normal) caution that may be required from everyone given the circumstances and nature of the case, reasonable doubts throughout the entire acquisitive prescription period whether the property or the right belonged to him. Good faith is no longer good faith if the possessor learns

205. Supreme Court Case No. 22 Cdo 1590/2001.
206. Section 1095 of the CC.

about facts that objectively must have raised doubts about the fact that the property lawfully belongs to him or that he is the subject of the right whose content he exercises.[207]

Good faith, however, is a mental state of the possessor – he believes that the right he exercises belongs to him, although this is not really the case. The fact whether a possessor is, given all circumstances, in good faith that a property or a right belongs to him must always be assessed objectively and not subjectively from the point of view (personal belief) of the possessor himself.[208] A possessor cannot be in good faith if he is subjectively convinced that a property or right belongs to him but he would have to know, had he maintained usual caution, that this is not the case.[209] One can imagine a case where possessors take possession based on an orally concluded contract because they are not aware of legislation. They could be subjectively convinced that they acquired the right of ownership in such a tract of land but objectively they cannot be convinced of this; had they maintained usual caution, they would have known that a valid legal title and registration in a public register are necessary for the acquisition of a right of ownership.

325. The case law of the Supreme Court is consistent that a right of ownership in a part of an adjacent tract of land may be acquired by prescription in a situation where the acquirer of the tract of land is wrong about the location of the ownership boundary as a result of which he also seizes possession of (a part of) the adjacent tract of land he considers to be part of the tract of land he was actually to acquire. In this case, circumstances accompanying the acquisition of the right of ownership and of the associated possession of the part of the adjacent land are decisive for the assessment of the possessor's good faith; it has to be evaluated whether the acquirer knew or, given the circumstances, should have known where the ownership boundary was located in the terrain.[210]

326. Therefore, for example, if possessors seize a small part of an adjacent tract of land in a belief that it is still part of their acquired tract of land with regard to the location of the fence, their good faith will not, in principle, be ruled out. In this respect, however, it is usually impossible to stipulate an unambiguous aspect for assessment of what ratio of areas of the purchased and actually possessed land rules out good faith of the acquirer that he only possesses the purchased land. According to case law, lawful possession cannot be ruled out even in cases where the acreage of the possessed land is up to 50% of the acreage of the purchased land, exceptionally even more (e.g., in the case of a land of an irregular shape in broken terrain or the possessor was mistaken by an expert[211]). If a possessor then seizes more than 50% of the acreage of the acquired land in excess, his good faith may be confirmed,

207. Supreme Court Case No. 22 Cdo 1843/2000; Supreme Court Case No. 22 Cdo 1806/2006.
208. Supreme Court Case No. 22 Cdo 1843/2000.
209. Constitutional Court Case No. ÚS III. ÚS 50/04.
210. Supreme Court Case No. 22 Cdo 1734/2015; Supreme Court Case No. 22 Cdo 81/2017.
211. Supreme Court Case No. 22 Cdo 1594/2004.

for example, in cases where the legal predecessor of the possessor was a close person who had donated the land to him, and the acquired and possessed lands constitute a single functional unit. In this respect, it will always have to be assessed individually whether the possessor could or could not have been in good faith.

327. What plays role in the assessment of good faith is especially the issue of distinctness of the ownership boundary in terrain, for example, the existence of boundary points, fence or wall, the question of extent of possession by legal predecessors, their confirmation of the location of the ownership boundary as well as the circumstance of family ties to the legal predecessor, existence of instruments that were available at the time of seizure of possession (in particular, a cadastral map, a plat map), the fact whether the acquired tract of land has been separated from the original land, the ratio of the acreage of the actually acquired land to the acreage of the possessed land as well as the attitude of the owner of the adjacent land to the possession of that part of his land.[212] On the contrary, what does not matter according to case law is the fact that the possessor did not pay tax on the part of the adjacent land possessed by him if he at the same time paid tax at least on the land actually acquired by him.[213] This reflects the fact that property tax is levied based on the information registered in the Land Register; it is apparent that if a possessor possesses, for example, a part of an adjacent land, a neighbour is registered for that land in the Land Register and the possessor is not obliged to tax.

328. Good faith is no longer good faith (and the acquisitive prescription period is interrupted) if the possessor learns about facts that objectively must have raised doubts about the fact that the property lawfully belongs to him or that he is the subject of the right whose content he exercises. It is not decisive whether the owner or, where applicable, another person informing the possessor of the actual ownership substantiate their claims. It is sufficient that their intervention is capable of making the possessor doubt the lawfulness of the possession.[214]

329. Therefore, a mere warning from a neighbour that the possessor possesses a part of a land in excess which does not belong to him is sufficient. It is not necessary to substantiate the legal fact based on which the neighbour acquired a right of ownership in the land or a copy of an entry in the Land Register.

330. Under CC 1964 lawful possession did not have to rely on an existing legal cause; a putative legal cause was sufficient.[215] An example may be seizure of possession of a part of an adjacent land whereby the possessor bases the possession on a legal fact (e.g., a contract) based on which he acquired his own land.[216]

212. For example, Supreme Court Case No. 22 Cdo 75/2016.
213. Supreme Court Case No. 22 Cdo 81/2017.
214. Supreme Court Case No. 22 Cdo 1339/2018.
215. Supreme Court Case No. 22 Cdo 1966/2005.
216. The case law of the Supreme Court distinguishes two types of land possession:

- First, it admits acquisitive prescription of a right of ownership in a tract of land whose possession was seized by the possessor in objective good faith that he acquired that land under

III. Acquisitive Prescription under the CC

331. The CC also provides for the institution of *acquisitive prescription* (sections 1089 et seq.). However, with regard to a relatively broad possibility of immediate acquisition of a right of ownership from a non-entitled person (in the case of immovable property subject to registration in public registers pursuant to section 984 of the CC), acquisitive prescription is rather a *subsidiary institution* of acquisition of a right of ownership; it will have its place especially where conditions of acquisition of a right of ownership in good faith from a non-entitled person are not met.

332. The CC now distinguishes *ordinary* (section 1089 of the CC) and *extraordinary* (section 1095 of the CC) acquisitive prescription. While ordinary acquisitive

---

a contract although that tract of land was not subject of the acquisition title. Acquisitive prescription, however, is in this case conceivable only exceptionally because absence of a tract of land in the acquisition title usually rules out that the possessor is in good faith given all circumstances (Supreme Court Case No. 22 Cdo 645/2014. This decision-making practice followed judgement of the Constitutional Court Case No. I. ÚS 2576/10, which concerned a case where a certain tract of land was not specified in the transfer contract but the Land Register Office registered the possessors as owners through its own mistake. The Constitutional Court held that if a state body registers possessors as owners of disputed tracts of land, it raises good faith in them in the correctness of such facts and in the act of the State itself.
Therefore, even if the disputed tracts of land were not expressly specified in the transfer contract, the possessors were in good faith that they had acquired the disputed lands into their ownership. Although they had not acquired them into their ownership through registration in the Land Register (they could not without a valid legal title), they were acquired by prescription. It follows that failure to specify real property in a contract makes in general (absolutely) good faith that the disputed real estate was transferred impossible.
What is decisive for the assessment of the possessor's objective good faith is in this case especially the circumstances related to the conclusion of the contract, i.e., in particular, the issue of genuine will of the parties, the issue why the tract of land that should have been the subject of the contract was not one in the end, how many plots of land should have been subject to the transfer, documents available during contract drafting, the issue who drafted the contract, and the issue how the parties acted (especially the acquirer); an essential circumstance is whether a right of ownership was registered in the Land Register under the contract (Supreme Court Case No. 22 Cdo 645/2014. In this example case, on the other hand, the ratio between the acreage of the tract of land acquired under the contract and the possessed tract of land is in principle not essential because the possessor bases his good faith not only in the error in the location of the ownership boundary of the tract of land he actually acquired but on the fact that he acquired the tract of land based on a contract although that tract of land was not specified in the contract.

- Second, the case law of the Supreme Court allows acquisitive prescription of a right of ownership in a part of an adjacent tract of land in a situation where the acquirer of the tract of land is wrong about the location of the ownership boundary as a result of which he also seizes possession of (a part of) the adjacent tract of land he considers to be part of the tract of land he was actually to acquire (cf. *see* above). What is decisive in this case for the assessment of the possessor's objective good faith is again the circumstances that accompanied the acquisition of the right of ownership and of the associated possession of the part of the adjacent tract of land; the circumstances, however, will not in this case not relate to whether the adjacent land was subject to the acquisition title but to the fact whether the acquirer knew or, given the circumstances, should have known where the ownership boundary is located (Supreme Court Case No. 22 Cdo 75/2016).

prescription requires a stricter qualification of possession but allows shorter acquisitive prescription periods, extraordinary acquisitive prescription, on the contrary, stipulates less strict conditions for qualification of possession but longer acquisitive prescription periods.

333. The new conception of acquisitive prescription is closely related to the new conception of possession. First, the new regulation only allows acquisitive prescription of rights, specifically ones that may be transferred to another by a legal act and that allow permanent or repeated performance.[217] Only such rights may be subject to possession. This includes, in particular, the right of ownership, easements and right of superficies, relating to tangible property. Obligational rights, in principle, may not be subject to acquisitive prescription although an opposite view has occasionally appeared in the literature.[218] Second, the CC also distinguishes between possession of a right of ownership and possession of other rights. Possession of a right of ownership is essentially possession of tangible property, and possession of another right is, for example, possession of a servitude. Third, the law defines three kinds of possession – lawful, in good faith and genuine – and their distinction plays an important role in the case of acquisitive prescription. The law stipulates a rebuttable presumption of a possession that is lawful, genuine and in good faith (section 994 of the CC), which divides the burden of proof between possible parties to a litigation in such a way that it will not be the possessor who has acquired a right of ownership by prescription who will bear the loss of the dispute if he fails to prove lawful, genuine and good-faith possession but the original owner who fails to prove that the possession was unlawful, non-genuine and in bad faith.

334. An *uninterrupted acquisitive prescription period* is required both in the case of ordinary and extraordinary acquisitive prescription. The acquisitive prescription period is interrupted if possession is not exercised for more than one year. There are cases where a possessor may not exercise the content of his possessed right, e.g., because the property is possessed by someone else. However, if the possessor seized possession within one year or successfully defended it by an action, the acquisitive prescription period would not be interrupted.

335. For the benefit of the person acquiring his right by prescription, the ordinary acquisitive prescription period also includes the period of lawful possession and *possession in good faith* by his predecessor.[219] This also applies to extraordinary acquisitive prescription, where the acquisitive prescription period of a predecessor in good faith will also be included.[220]

336. In certain cases, an acquisitive prescription period does not even commence or does not continue while a certain fact lasts – e.g., marriage (an acquisitive

217. Section 988(1) of the CC.
218. Jan Petrov in Petrov, Výtisk, Beran, *Občanský zákoník*, 1094.
219. Section 1092 of the CC.
220. Section 1096 of the CC.

prescription period does not commence or continue between spouses while the marriage lasts). This applies by analogy to persons living in a common household, a legal representative and the person represented, guardian and ward, and tutor and person under tutorship.[221]

A. *Ordinary Acquisitive Prescription*

337. Ordinary acquisitive prescription requires lawful, genuine and in good faith possession of a right eligible for acquisitive prescription. In the case of tracts of land, possession must last ten years. In relation to tracts of land, one may consider cases where the material publicity of public registers (Land Register) does not apply, that is, for example, where a right of ownership is acquired gratuitously from a person registered in the Land Register who is not the actual owner or where acquisition takes place otherwise than based on a legal act (cf. Part III, Chapter 3). It can, therefore, be assumed that lawful acquisitive prescription will be rather an exception because most cases where the acquirer acquires possession that is lawful, genuine and in good faith will be subject to immediate protection of acquirer in good faith.[222,223]

B. *Extraordinary Acquisitive Prescription*

338. By law, extraordinary acquisitive prescription does not require lawful or genuine possession or possession in good faith. The subject of acquisitive prescription must be, of course, a right eligible for acquisitive prescription, but in addition to that, only the absence of an unfair intention of the possessor and the expiry of an acquisitive prescription period (twenty years for tracts of land) are sufficient.

339. Extraordinary acquisitive prescription will be more common in practice than ordinary one.[224]

340. Extraordinary acquisitive prescription does not require lawful possession. This means that it allows acquisition of a right of ownership by prescription even to

221. Section 1098 of the CC.
222. Section 984 of the CC.
223. The following situation is an example of ordinary acquisitive prescription: Following an advertisement published on the internet, the acquirer acquires a book from the transferor under a valid purchase contract. However, it is subsequently found that the book had been stolen. Since in this case it is not possible to acquire property from a non-entitled person immediately (s. 1111 of the CC), the acquirer may acquire a right of ownership through ordinary acquisitive prescription in three years if he is at the same time a genuine possessor in good faith.
224. The following situation is an example of extraordinary acquisitive prescription: A buyer purchased a tract of land with an acreage of 230 m^2. He started using the tract of land as it was fenced. It was subsequently found that he was using 20 m^2 in excess of what he had bought, i.e., that he was using a part of an adjacent tract of land. He could acquire a right of ownership of the part of the adjacent tract of land with acreage 20 m^2 under the conditions of extraordinary acquisitive prescription (i.e., after twenty years of possession unless an unfair intention can be objected).

a possessor who has an invalid or no legal acquisition title or cannot prove one. However, a possessor who has an unfair intention cannot acquire property by prescription. It is obvious that an unfair intention is not the same as possession in bad faith.

Given the fact that extraordinary acquisitive prescription rules out an unfair intention of the possessor, one can presume that possession without such an intention, i.e., possession in a belief that it does not harm anybody, will suffice.[225] That means that a certain degree of fairness of the possessor is necessary for extraordinary acquisitive prescription; however, he will not be assessed as strictly as in the case of possession in good faith, which is a prerequisite of ordinary acquisitive prescription.

341. Extraordinary acquisitive prescription will be relatively common in practice because it will aim at cases of possession of parts 'added by fencing' (cf. above). In all these cases, possessors do not have valid legal titles to them, that is, they possess them without a legal cause. Acquisitive prescription will, therefore, be possible even in the case of possession '*contra tabulas*', i.e., one contrary to the state in a public register. In principle, the CC noticeably does not allow possession in good faith contrary to the state in a public register, and a possessor, maintaining the necessary degree of caution, must know the plot number of the possessed plot of land; good faith is ruled out if a different person is registered as its owner. However, it is hard to conclude that after the conditions of such acquisitive prescription are met, the person who has acquired a right of ownership by prescription will be a possessor in bad faith, which also applies to other cases of ownership possession if the actual state is contrary to the state in the Land Register.[226] Moreover, the principle that ignorance of information registered in a public register is no excuse[227] does not apply to the cadastral map but only to information about rights. However the land boundary may be visible in the cadastral map, it may be often problematic to determine it in the terrain, which applies especially to steep terrains, special layout of tracts of land, etc.

342. The Supreme Court has already had a chance to touch upon extraordinary acquisitive prescription in its decision-making practice. It was a case where possession had lasted for more than fifty years, and extraordinary acquisitive prescription would apply to that case under the new legislation unless an unfair intention was proven – the burden of proof is borne by the original owner, not the possessor.[228] The Supreme Court has also ruled that possession lasting undisturbed for (at least) thirty-five years can be seen similarly.

---

225. Jiří Spáčil in Jiří Spáčil et al., *Občanský zákoník,* 63.
226. *Ibid.*
227. Section 980(1) of the CC.
228. Supreme Court Case No. 22 Cdo 2520/2011.

Chapter 4. Accession

§1. Introduction

343. An accession (*přírůstek*) is an addition to property, something that becomes its part and is not a separate subject of a right of ownership; it only becomes one if it is separated from the principal property (e.g., fruits of trees, young animals). Some accessions, however, cannot be separated this way (immovable structures on a tract of land, trees already rooted in the soil) and they become part of the property they acceded to.

344. Czech law distinguishes between *natural accessions*, resulting from the action of nature, *artificial accessions*, caused by man, and *mixed accessions*, which are a combination of the previous two.

345. Natural accessions of property are mainly its fruits; these are part of fruit-bearing property and are not a separate subject of a right of ownership; they become one only after separation from the principal property. Natural accessions of immovable property are also alluvium and tear-off;[229] together with them, the law also provides for a case where an island is formed by the action of the waterflow; these are cases the practice has not been encountering very often lately, probably as a result of control of watercourses.

346. Legislation is based on the following principles:

- If there is a change in the appearance and shape of a tract of land by action of water, the right of ownership in the tract of lands remains unaffected. Therefore, a watercourse bed created by tear-off or as a result of an island being formed remains in the ownership of the owner of the original bed.
- If soil is gradually drifted, the alluvium becomes part of the coastal land, and the owner of the coastal land (*alluvio*) acquires a right of ownership *ipso iure*.
- In the case of drifting of larger pieces of soil (that are part of another land), the same rule as for alluvium applies; however, the owner of the coastal land acquires a right of ownership only if the owner of the soil fails to exercise his right within one year of drifting (*avulsio*).
- If a watercourse separates a part of a tract of land as an island (therefore, there is no drifting on a land of another), the owner of the original land is the owner of the island.

347. Artificial accessions of property are created by processing, mixing, construction or encroachment.

New property is created by processing immovable property if the processed property cannot be restored to the previous state or can be restored only at a significant

229. Sections 1068 through 1071 of the CC.

loss or with a substantial loss. Processing differs from mixing, where restoration of the previous state is not possible but the whole can be divided into parts without interference with the substance.

348. A mixed accession is sowing of a land with seeds of another or planting with plants of another; the owner of the land is entitled to what accedes this way. The landowner's right of ownership in plants as parts of land is created at the moment of rooting.

§2. Acquisition of a Right of Ownership in Fruits and Revenues of Property

349. A *fruit* is what property regularly provides by its inherent nature, as follows from and is appropriate to its usual intended purpose, whether or not as a result of the endeavour of man (e.g., an apple fallen from a tree).[230] Traditionally, there was a distinction between natural and legal fruits (e.g., property revenue, interest on deposits); the CC refers to the latter as property revenues: 'Revenues are what property regularly provides by its legal nature.'[231]

350. Until a fruit is separated from the parental property, it follows its legal fate as its component. Right of ownership in a fruit is acquired originally by separation, at the moment the fruit separates from the paternal property. Ownership of a separated fruit is acquired originally by the owner of the fruit-bearing property, its possessor in good faith or the obligee from the servitude of right of usufruct.

351. Obligees (e.g., usufructuary lessee) acquire the fruits of property by perception (harvesting, gripping the fruit), i.e., derivatively.[232]

§3. Acquisition of a Right of Ownership as a Result of Property Processing

352. *Processing* is the creation of new property; there is a change in the purpose or economic function and usability of the existing movable property by work of man.[233] Frequently, the designation of property also changes. Processing is a real act, not a legal act.

---

230. Section 491(1) of the CC.
231. Section 1072 of the CC.
232. In the prevailing view of Czech law, even an obligee from a servitude acquires ownership of fruits by separation, not perception (i.e., harvest) – *see* Jan Sedláček, *Vlastnické právo* (Prague: Nákladem právnického knihkupectví a nakladatelství V. Linhart, 1935, reprint Wolters Kluwer 2012), 252.
233. According to case law, processing is usage of material with the purpose of creating a new thing for oneself – cf. Supreme Court Case No. 2 Cdon 1312/1996. The CC apparently does not regulate specification, i.e., transformation of matter of another to a different thing that would establish a right of ownership for the creator. It is always required that several things of distinct owners be

The rules on processing do not apply where there is an agreement of the parties as to whom the newly created thing will belong (e.g., a contract of employment or a contract for work).

353. Processing need not in any way affect the right of ownership in things being processed if their owner is one person. The owner of the new thing becomes the owner of the original things. This also applies if processing is not carried out by the owner of the things but by another person on behalf of the owner.

354. There are no special problems even in cases where two (and more) things of different owners are processed and these things can be separated and restored to the original state without damaging. In such a case, every person involved remains the owner of his thing.[234]

355. Problematic can be solution of situations where things of different owners are processed that cannot be restored to the previous state either at all or only with a substantial loss.

In these cases, the right of ownership in the original thing (things) is extinguished and a right of ownership in the newly created thing is created. The assessment of who will become the owner of the new thing is in principle based on the aspect of value of the result. The owner of a newly created thing is the person whose material or work made the largest contribution to the result.[235] This owner, however, is obliged to make settlement with the owner of the thing that has been processed by compensating the value of the processed thing and remunerating the person who has not become an owner for his work. If it is impossible to identify an owner of a new thing, the thing becomes co-owned by the owners of the processed things. The shares are determined according to the values of the processed things.[236] If shares cannot be determined this way, equality of shares applies (section 1076 of the CC). These rules, however, are only applicable if the processor was in good faith (i.e., he did not and could not know he was processing a thing of another).[237] If the processor was not in good faith, the owner of the thing has the right to appropriate the thing or require compensation. This right of choice lapses (is extinguished) after one month from the date the owner became aware of the processing.

---

joined. On the other hand, in this case the owner of the newly created property may be also the person whose work made the largest contribution (s. 1074(1) of the CC).

234. The right to request rendition of a joined thing, however, is not an action for the recovery of a thing – it differs in that the defendant does not have in his control the plaintiff's property but something else which is yet to be transformed into a thing that can be rendered – cf. Jiří Krčmář, *Práva věcná* (Prague: 1946, reprint 2014), 268.

235. Section 1074(1) of the CC.

236. The CC does not take into account the value of work – Petra Joana Pipková in Petrov, Výtisk, Beran, *Občanský zákoník*, 1074.

237. The criterion of good faith was elaborated on by case law already before 1 Jan. 2014 – cf. Supreme Court Case No. 29 Odo 1350/2005.

356. Even in the case of a mere repair, the rules on processing will apply; the owner of the principal property acquires a right of ownership in the repair of a used thing of another (component) (section 1077 of the CC). The thing being repaired does not become a new thing; therefore, the owner does not change. This rule applies to cases where an indivisibly joined or processed thing or work has a significantly lower value than the principal thing. The owner of the repaired thing is obliged to reimburse its owner for the value of the processed thing.

If it is possible to restore a thing to the original state, the owner of the component may request its separation.

§4. Acquisition of a Right of Ownership as a Result of Mixing

357. *Mixing* is accumulating and blending of things of different owners that can no longer be distinguished from each other. If it is possible to identify mixed things, there are no special problems, each owner retains his/her ownership in those things. However, impossibility to restore the original state does not give rise to co-ownership but a right of the owners to separate a proportional part of what has been created by mixing (recovery of quantity) or to require compensation. This right of choice lapses (is extinguished) after one month from the date the owner became aware of the mixing.

358. The person who has a thing in his possession has a detention right in it until the owner pays compensation to him.

If things of the same kind are mixed that cannot be distinguished and separated, the owners of mixed things become co-owners. Each owns a proportional part of the mixed things (section 1079 of the CC).[238] If it is not possible to determine proportional parts, the person who mixed the things acquires exclusive ownership (an action for recovery is inadmissible here).[239]

It is important for the amount of compensation whether the person who mixed the things did so in good faith; if he was not in good faith, his position in the decision-making about the mixed thing, or specifically about the provision of compensation for it, is less advantageous.[240]

If a third party was involved in the mixing who was not in good faith, the third party will also compensate the owners, in addition to actual damage in excess of what they have not been compensated for under the foregoing principles, for lost profits.

238. For example, each of two persons pours 50 litres of their wine in a barrel. Both acquire a right of ownership in the proportional part (half) of the mixture.
239. Section 1041(2) of the CC.
240. Sections 1080, 1082 of the CC.

§5. Acquisition of a Right of Ownership in Structures; Encroachment

359. Under the *superficies solo cedit* rule, a structure is, in principle, part of the land and 'accedes' to the land, or specifically to its owner. It is not decisive what material a structure has been built of (whether one's own or of another person) and whether the builder was in good or bad faith. The aforementioned facts, however, have an impact on the settlement of mutual relationships between the builder and the landowner. This means that if a structure is part of a tract of land, it is not possible to acquire a right of ownership in it separately. Only the tract of land may be subject to legal acts and ownership, and the legal regime of the tract of land automatically applies to the structure as its component.

360. The previous legislation in CC 1964 was based on the principle that structures are not part of land on which they are erected and are, therefore, separate property. The current CC (since 1 January 2014) departed from an opposite conception and, on the contrary, made structures (in general) directly part of land on which they are located. The superficial principle is stipulated in section 506 of the CC typically for structures erected after 1 January 2014. The reintroduction of the *superficies solo cedit* in the regime of section 506 does not, in principle, retroactively affect legal relationships created while CC 1964 was in effect. There is a separate and comprehensive group of statutory provisions for these cases that have to be followed (sections 3054 through 3060 of the CC). Although this is a group of transitional provisions, which gives an impression of their temporary applicability, the real estate practice will be dealing with them for several decades. The up-to-dateness of these rules is based, among other things, on the fact that at the end of 2013, of a total of approximately 4,000,000 structures, there were approximately 350,000 structures on tracts of land of another. The basic rule departs from the fact that a structure that was not, under CC 1964, part of the tract of land on which it is erected ceases to be separate property on the date of the CC coming into effect (i.e., 1 January 2014) and becomes part of the land – however, provided that the owner of the structure and of the tract of land as of 1 January 2014 was the same person.

361. An opposite principle applies to cases where the same person is not the owner of the structure and of the land on 1 January 2014, i.e., the ownership regime of the land and of the structure firmly attached to the tract of land will be different. In these cases, the different ownership regime is maintained and the structure does not become part of the land; it retains its nature of a separate immovable property.[241] The law does not in any way limit the time frame for which this state may last. The CC, however, seeks to unify the ownership regime of the structure and of the tract of land. It does so in section 3056 by providing the owner of the tract of land with an *ex lege* pre-emptive right in the structure and the owner of the structure with an *ex lege* right in the tract of land.

362. If the owner of the structure differs from the owner of the tract of land as of 1 January 2014 but the owner of the structure becomes the owner of the tract of

241. Supreme Court Case No. 22 Cdo 480/2015.

land after that date (or vice versa), the structure ceases to be a separate property and becomes part of the tract of land it has been erected on. This principle, however, does not apply in cases where a structure is not part of the respective tract of land under the now effective CC (e.g., an underground structure with a separate intended purpose – cf. Part I, Chapter 1, §1, II). Even in this case there is no limitation as to when the superficial principal has to be fulfilled.

363. In some cases, a builder who has in good faith built over a small part of an adjacent tract of land of another with a small part of his structure (encroachment[242]) acquires a right of ownership in the covered part of the tract of land; it accedes the tract of land owned by the builder.

§6. Acquisition of a Right of Ownership as a Result Sowing a Tract of Land

364. Sowing of a tract of land is a kind of mixed accession. This concerns artificially planted plants or artificial sowing, i.e., with the endeavour of man, not naturally (e.g., by wind). Plants which become part of the tract of land 'accede' to the landowner regardless of whether they grew from seeds or were planted and regardless of who sowed or planted, whether legitimately or not or whom the seeds or seedlings belonged to. The landowner, however, is obliged to provide compensation for the seeds and plants according to the rules applicable to structures on the land of another.[243] This means that a landowner who has used seeds or plants of another in good faith will compensate their current owner with the usual price of seeds or plants. If the landowner was not in good faith, he will also compensate lost profits and actual damage if these are not covered by the compensation for the value of the seeds and plants. If the person who sowed or planted the land was in good faith, he is entitled to compensation of reasonably incurred costs, otherwise he has the rights of obligations of an agent without mandate.

242. Section 1087 of the CC, which also applies, pursuant to s. 3059, to structures erected before 1 Jan. 2014.
243. Sections 1083 and 1084 of the CC.

Chapter 5. Appropriation

365. Appropriation is acquisition of a right of ownership by direct seizure of possession of immovable property that does not belong to anyone with the intent of acquisition of a right of ownership in it.

366. Property that does not belong to anyone (*res nullius*) is property abandoned by its owner with the intent of no longer having it for himself. Property is considered abandoned if its owner does not exercise his right of ownership for three years in the case of movable property and for ten years in the case of immovable property.[244] Abandoned real estate may not be freely occupied, and it always falls into state ownership.

367. Although animals are not things under the CC, the provisions on ownership and acquisition of ownership apply to them by analogy.[245] Appropriation of animals is regulated separately. A masterless animal may be appropriated under stipulated conditions. The legal regime differs according to whether animals are wild, tamed or captive.

368. Wild animals living in the wild are, in principle, masterless. Relatively broad restrictions on appropriation of such animals are stipulated in special regulations. Such regulation is contained, for example, in Act No. 449/2001 Sb., on Gamekeeping, or Act No. 99/2004 Sb., on Fishery.[246]

Tamed animals are wild animals that as a species usually live in the wild as in their natural habitat but an individual may live with a human, e.g., because it was raised that way since young or was gradually domesticated. If such animals become free, do not return to the owner in a reasonable period (six weeks) and the owner does not pursue them, they become masterless animals.

Captive animals are wild animals someone has appropriated. Such animals have a natural instinct to become free. If they become free and their owner fails to promptly and consistently pursue or search for them in an attempt to recapture them, they, in principle, become masterless animals, unless they were marked in a way that it is possible to find out who their owner is.

244. Section 1050 of the CC.
245. Section 494 of the CC.
246. The right of gamekeeping involving the right of hunting may be exercised only in a hunting ground, which is a set of contiguous hunting tracts of land of one or more owners defined in a decision of the state administration of gamekeeping, in which the right of gamekeeping under the Gamekeeping Act can be exercised. Gamekeeping may be performed by the holder of the hunting ground, which is in principle a person who has received recognition of the hunting ground by a decision of a state administration of gamekeeping. Therefore, a right of ownership in a hunting land alone is not sufficient – cf. Supreme Court Case No. 22 Cdo 3006/2000.

A *domesticated animal* is an animal whose species lives with humans and do not live free in the wild – either at all or exceptionally. Such animals can be considered abandoned if circumstances clearly show the owner's intention to get rid of or drive off the animal.[247]

369. The distinction between the aforementioned categories of animals is also important from the point of view of persons eligible for appropriation. While wild, captive and abandoned domestic animals may be appropriated by anyone regardless of on what tract of land they are, tamed animals may be appropriated on a private tract of land only by its owner and on a public property by anyone.

370. There are exceptions for animals kept in a zoo and fish in a pond or a similar facility which is not public property. Such animals cannot be considered masterless.[248]

---

247. For example, if an owner of a cat takes the cat to the forest and releases it into the wild. It is possible to infer an obvious intention of the owner to get rid of the cat from such a circumstance. The cat becomes masterless and anyone can appropriate it.
248. Section 1049 of the CC.

Chapter 6. Expropriation

§1. Use of Owner's Property in an Emergency or Urgent Public Interest

371. In an *emergency situation or urgent public interest*, owner's property may be used for the period and to the extent necessary if the purpose cannot be achieved otherwise.[249] This allows to ad hoc restrict the owner's right of ownership by using his property under specified conditions. A temporary, not permanent restriction and absence of previous proceedings are presumed. This is a kind of material expropriation.[250]

372. What can be considered an emergency or urgent public interest in a particular case depends on the judge's discretion in that particular case. Emergencies will be mainly situations caused by natural disasters (floods, earthquakes, etc.) directly endangering the lives or health of persons but not – with infrequent exceptions – another urgent (e.g., property-related) interest. Situations of urgent public interest may also result from, for example, natural disasters and a public interest may be fulfilled not only in the case of threat to health or lives of persons but also to their property; this can, however, also include cases where it is necessary to use certain property to satisfy the needs of the public – for example, case law has concluded that urgent public interest can also be seen in a need to use a tract of land as a public space if it has not been expropriated for these purposes.[251] However, the situation of the acting person, the effectiveness of the use of the property including the seriousness of the impending consequence have to be taken into account both in the case of emergency and urgent public interest.

373. However, the owner's property may only be used for the necessary time. The necessary time means a period necessary precisely and only to achieve the purpose of usage of the property, that is, to avert or alleviate an emergency or fulfil urgent public interest. After achieving the purpose the use of the property aimed at, the property must be returned to the owner without delay. Property of another must be used in a manner that least interferes with its essence and functionality and does not unreasonably reduce its value. The use of property of another in an emergency or urgent public interest must be seen as *ultima ratio*. Therefore, if an emergency can be alleviated or urgent public interest can be fulfilled by other (milder) means than the use of owner's property (e.g., by using one's own property or by intervention of emergency services), these must be used even if their use was less comfortable.

374. The owner is entitled to full compensation for the use of his property as stipulated in section 1039. The amount of compensation for the use of the property must take into account the time and degree of limitation of the right of ownership.

249. Section 1037 of the CC.
250. Special regulation may be foreseen by special regulations.
251. Supreme Court Case No. 32 Odo 823/2003; Supreme Court Case No. 28 Cdo 1127/2009.

In the case of damage or destruction of property, the usual price of the property is used (cf. section 492(1)); however, other immediate costs are also reimbursed. The person liable to provide compensation is the person in whose benefit the property was reasonably used, even if it was used by someone else.[252] In the case of use of property in urgent public interest, compensation will be provided depending on the circumstances of the case by the relevant public entity concerned by the matter.

§2. EXPROPRIATION

375. The right of ownership may be limited or property expropriated only in *the public interest* which cannot be satisfied otherwise, and solely by means of a statute and for compensation.[253] The right of ownership may be limited or property expropriated only by a public expropriation decision issued based on a statutory formal procedure (formal expropriation) or directly based on law (legal expropriation). The constitutional basis is stipulated in Article 11(4) of the CFRF and Articles 17 and 18 of the European Convention on Human Rights and Article 1 of the Additional Protocol. In principle, expropriation cannot be achieved by other means.

376. Expropriation is understood as a *forced extinction of the right of ownership* (or of any other private right which is as such also subject to the right of ownership) of the current owner; he is completely deprived of his right of ownership, so he cannot exercise any of his ownership entitlements. The entity in whose benefit the expropriation took place (expropriator) acquires the right of ownership originally. The title for the acquisition of the right of ownership in the expropriated property on the side of the expropriator is an expropriation decision.

377. In addition to expropriation, the right of ownership (or another private right) may be limited, which must be understood as a forced termination of some of entitlements of the owner or, where applicable, establishment of certain entitlements in favour of third parties. This may include, for example, declaration of a protected area on the owner's tract of land or declaration of owner's property on a cultural monument.

378. Expropriation is possible only in the public interest, that is, in the case of a specific public need. Expropriation is permissible only for the purpose stipulated by a special regulation. It may be inferred from the nature of the matter that it is an interest that can be described as public or publicly beneficial or an interest of the society as a whole. For example, construction of a public road or creation and operation of an electricity transmission system is in the public interest.[254]

252. Jiří Večeřa in Jiří Švestka, Jan Dvořák & Josef Fiala et al., *Občanský zákoník. Komentář. III. díl* (Prague: Wolters Kluwer 2009), 294.
253. Section 1038 of the CC.
254. Supreme Court Case No. 21 Cdo 799/2016.

379. The requirement of *ultima ratio* is reflected in two facts. First, the expropriated property must be capable of fulfilling a public need. Second, fulfilment of public interest may not be achieved otherwise (by milder means), that is, for example, by agreement between the parties involved or using other property owned by the person in whose favour the expropriation is to take place.

380. The process of expropriation, or limitation of the right of ownership, must be preceded by proceedings that must provide guarantees of legality, including space for the owner to protect his interests. In the event of the absence of special regulation, the proceedings are governed by Expropriation Act (EA). The expropriation authority is the municipal office of a municipality with extended competence or a metropolitan authority in the administrative district of which the tract of land or structure in question is located. Expropriation is only permissible for the purpose of expropriation stipulated in a special law and only if the public interest in achieving such purpose outweighs the preservation of the existing rights of the person whose property is being expropriated. Expropriation titles defined by special laws, therefore, primarily enshrine the purpose that is to be achieved through exercise of the expropriation title. Legislation also provides for judicial review of expropriation or limitation of the right of ownership by a decision in expropriation proceedings.

381. For a limitation of the right of ownership or expropriation of property, the owner is entitled to full *compensation* corresponding to the extent to which his property has been affected by those measures. In principle, compensation is provided in money. However, it may also be provided in a different way, if so stipulated by the parties.[255] However, an entitlement to compensation for a limitation of the right of ownership does not arise in the case of any limitation of the right of ownership but only where the limitation reaches such an intensity that the very essence of ownership is affected.[256]

382. Since it is not possible to award compensation by reinstatement, it is necessary to ensure such compensation for the person whose property has been expropriated that the property status of that person before and after the expropriation will be the same. Compensation must be determined taking into account all individual circumstances while using objective criteria, i.e., abstract possibilities of use of the property. The entity obliged to provide compensation is the entity in whose favour the limitation is made, that is, in the case of interest of the society, the obliged entity is the state.[257]

383. The basis for the determination of the amount of compensation is the usual price of the tract of land or structure including their accessories in the case of

255. Section 1039 of the CC.
256. Supreme Court Case No. 22 Cdo 367/2012; Supreme Court Case No. 22 Cdo 3188/2012; Supreme Court Case No. 22 Cdo 3877/2012.
257. Constitutional Court Case No. II. ÚS 2520/15.

removal of the right of ownership in them, or from the price of a right corresponding to an easement in the case of limitation of the right of ownership in a tract of land or a structure by establishing an easement or if a right corresponding to an easement has been removed or limited.[258] In the case of immovable property, the compensation must also include costs that had to be expended at the time of expropriation so that the person whose property is being expropriated obtained an immovable property of the same kind as well as all associated costs incurred directly in connection with the expropriation or limitation of the right of ownership (e.g., the cost of entry of the right of ownership of the newly acquired immovable property in the Land Register, relocation costs, costs associated with a loss of place of business and other similar costs).[259]

258. Section 10(1) of the EA.
259. Eva Dobrovolná in Petrov, Výtisk, Beran, *Občanský zákoník*, 1112.

Chapter 7. Insolvency

384. The sale of movable and immovable property from the debtor's estate has certain specificities. An advantage of purchase of estate from insolvency proceedings is a high legal certainty that property purchased from the receiver will not be encumbered with any pledge or enforcement after the sale because the effects of pledges or enforcements by sale of property from insolvency proceedings are extinguished by law.[260] The sale of such property is overseen by representatives of the debtor's creditor or the pledgee as well as an insolvency court – the receiver usually maintains special accounts for the receipt of the purchase price, which ensures that the funds on those accounts will not be used in violation of their purpose.

385. Property in insolvency proceedings may be acquired through auction or outside auction. The receiver will decide on the method of sale of the estate under paragraph 1 with the consent of the committee of creditors.

386. Primarily, property from the estate may be acquired in a *public auction.*[261]
A public auction is carried out by an auctioneer at the request of the receiver. The right of ownership is acquired at the moment of fall of the hammer under the condition that the price achieved in the auction has been paid in the stipulated time limit.
Moreover, it is possible to conduct an auction of movable and immovable property before the competent district court pursuant to provisions of the CPC. A motion for such sale is submitted by the receiver, who is the only party to the proceedings.[262] Also here, the right of ownership is acquired at the moment of fall of the hammer under the condition that the price achieved in the auction has been paid in the stipulated time limit. The auction, however, is carried out by a court or a bailiff.
A similar regime is also foreseen where the auction is carried out by a judicial executor according to the Enforcement Procedure Code (EPC).[263]

387. Sale *outside auction* is carried out by the receiver with the consent of the insolvency court and the committee of creditors. When consent is granted, the insolvency court may stipulate conditions for the sale. The acquirer acquires the right of ownership based on a contract of sale, and real estate also requires an entry in the Land Register.

388. Where an enterprise is sold in this manner, all rights and obligations subject to the sale pass to the acquirer, including rights and obligations arising from labour relationships with employees of the debtor's enterprise, with the exception of claims against the debtor arisen until the date of effect of the contract.[264]

260. Section 285(1)(b) of the IA.
261. Act No. 26/2000 Sb., on Public Auctions.
262. Section 288 of the IA.
263. Act No. 120/2001 Sb., EPC.
264. Section 291 of the IA.

Part IV. Trust and Fiduciary Mechanisms

Chapter 1. Administration of Property. *Fiducia cum Amico*

§1. INTRODUCTION

389. As part of the recodification of private law, the CC introduced some truly groundbreaking changes into the Czech legal system, modifying both its conceptual framework and content. While some of those changes mark a return to traditional concepts of continental law that had been abandoned during the socialist times, others reflect the current shifts in the society to which the law needs to respond.

390. When viewed from the perspective of more stable legal systems found in Western Europe, the extent of the changes may appear as hard to understand or even be found inconceivable.[265]

The new Czech private law, being the result of discussions lasting for over ten years, represents a legal regulation occurring not on the basis of any long-term doctrinal and case law tradition, but a jump return to European traditions with a conscious declaration of discontinuity (although not complete) not only with the 'socialist rule of law' governing the pre-1989 era, but also with its partially reformed 'post-velvet-revolution' continuation.

391. To a large extent, it thus represents a certain step into the unknown, when the performance of the new law 'in action' may only be predicted with a substantial degree of uncertainty. This reflection also applies to such fundamental issues as the interpretation of legal transactions or their validity and effectiveness. Probably the most significant conceptual change is strengthening of the autonomy of the individual's will and the increased possibility to live 'one's own way'.[266]

392. What is even less predictable is obviously the reaction of the Czech law, as a representative of the *civil law* tradition, to a concept that is essentially foreign to it – such as the *trust* based on the Anglo-American legal tradition. In terms of theoretical reflections, one may fear the worst confusion and uncertainty. Nevertheless,

265. However, that is not that exceptional in Central and Eastern Europe. *See* Petr Lavický in Jan Hurdík et al., *Private Law Reform* (Munipress, 2014).

266. From 1 Jan. 2014, the following are in effect: the CC, the ABC, the International Private Law Act No. 91/2012 Coll., as well as many other laws. The key element is expressed in s. 3, subs. 1 of the CC: '*private law protects the dignity and freedom of the person as well as his natural right to pursue his own happiness and that of his family in a manner that does not unduly harm others*'.

a large amount of practical experience shows that if a certain legal regulation is functional enough, the legal practice lacks any significant motivation to deal with the reflections on its conceptual basis, and referring to these issues is found mainly on the pages of dissertations. In this respect, the Czech law will function as 'an interesting laboratory'[267] whose results will possibly be of interest not only to its addressees but also to the legal science.

393. The trust fund (*svěřenský fond*)[268] represents a new specific tool for administration of property which has been subject to some quite emotional discussions since its introduction. In the main part, the regulation follows the model found in the law of Québec.[269] However, since the Québec model was not adopted word for word, the applicability to the Czech legal context of the conclusions of the legal doctrine and judicial decisions relating to trust/fiducia in Québec is limited.

394. What was introduced into Czech law is an instrument that conceptually stems from the tradition of common law. It is not yet certain whether the 'body' of the Czech legal system will accept or, rather, reject the trust fund. At this point it seems that it is likely to survive.

395. The Czech '*trust-like*' legal regulation is currently only five years old. There is not much practical experience in the application practice. For this reason, we prefer to provide an outline of the new legal regulation in the text below, pointing out certain reflections initiated by this legal regulation so far. Only the future will show to what extent these outlines will be preserved.

§2. Administration of Property of Others

I. Administration of Property of Others: Conceptual Framework, Basic Elements

396. During the recodification of Czech private law (effective from 1 January 2014), new regulations were incorporated into the CC (Part III, Segment 6, sections 1440 et seq.) concerning the administration of the property of others and the formation and operation of *trust funds* ('svěřenský fond' in Czech) *as a special trust-like instrument* applicable for the administration of property (or assets) as separate from its owner. As stated above, the inspiration for these innovations came from the legal regulation in the QCC (in effect from 1994), which made the attempt to effectively transplant the common law institute of the trust into the context of continental private law.

267. For more details, *see* Vlastimil Pihera, *Nejpodivnější zvíře v lese – poznámky ke svěřenskému fondu* (Obchodně právní revue, Vol. 10/2012), 278 et seq.
268. Sections 1448 et seq. CC.
269. Sections 1260–1298 QCC.

397. The main reason for including this regulation within Part III of the CC, which deals with absolute property rights, is likely to have been the fact that the *trust fund* is formed by *autonomous assets*, i.e., it is *a specific form of ownership without an owner*. The other regulations concerning the administration of the property of others are likewise related to administered property regardless of whether such assets are administered on a contractual basis or due to some other legal reason. The administration of the property of others, however, does not constitute any special absolute right (right in rem).

398. The placement of the regulation of the administration of the property of others among absolute property rights may, at first sight, give rise to *an impression of its mandatory character*. Relations arising in connection with such administration, however, usually have a contractual nature (i.e., they operate exclusively *inter partes*). Thus, it may be assumed that the legal regulation of such relations is directory (dispositive) due to its subject matter. The legal framework is set in a mandatory manner only where the legal relations have effects towards third parties (section 978 of CC).

399. The reason for the regulation of the property of others (in sections 1400 et seq. of CC) is to provide *ancillary rights for the administration of the property of others,* mainly with respect to the special regulation of the trust fund. This concerns, above all, a flexible set of general rules governing the rights and obligations of an administrator of the property of others towards the property that he or she administers. In other words, neither any special right (right in rem) is being conceived here nor any limitation of the application of such rules to a pre-defined list of legal relations is being intended.

400. The main feature of the 'administration of property' that *distinguishes* the administration of property of others from, for instance, an escrow or a simple instruction, is the *administrator's autonomous position* during the exercise of his or her powers, i.e., *the discretionary nature of such an activity*. The administrator is always, to a bigger or lesser extent as delimited by the purpose of the administration, authorised as well as simultaneously obliged to decide at his or her own discretion.

401. As a result, the delimitation of the specific features of the administration of the property of others needs to be sought primarily beyond the actual wording of the law.[270] Since the issue is intentionally open to interpretation, the law does not aim to be conclusive in this matter.

---

270. Madeleine Cantin Cumyn, *L'administration du bien d'autri. Traité de droit civil* (Montréal: Lés Editions Yvon Blais Inc., 2000), 51.

II. The Extent of Application of Rules for Administration of Property of Others

402. The very concept of '*the property of others*' ('*cizí majetek*' in Czech) implies the existence of property that does not belong to the administrator. On the basis of a specific legal reason, the administrator is involved in relations concerning a thing that the administrator has no ownership rights to.

403. Since no agreement has been achieved in the Czech legal doctrine so far on the extent of the application of the rules for the administration of the property of others, one can come across various constructions. At one end of the imaginary scale of opinions there are supporters of the restrictive approach, under which the regulation of the administration of the property of others in the CC should be applied only where the law or a contract refer to the rules for the administration of property in an explicit manner. At the other end of the scale there are proponents of the extensive approach, under which the rules for the administration of the property of others should be applied in all situations when some property is being administered by someone for some specific purpose (including, for instance, the administration of a shared thing). In this context, it cannot be foreseen with any degree of certainly which of those positions will prevail in the Czech legal doctrine in the future.

404. As regards the issue of what form of obligation relation the regulation of the administration of the property of others in the CC will be applied to, one must consider not only the general meaning of the concept of administration of the property of others *but also the nature of each particular obligation* that is subject to our consideration and to the legal regulation of that obligation. That is because not every legal relation that may be generally characterised as administration of the property of others is actually subject to the legal regulation of the administration of the property of others as provided for in Part III, Segment 6 of the CC. Paradoxically, some legal relations that do not, *stricto sensu*, meet the general elements defining the administration of the property of others, are actually subject to it.

405. Some situations meeting the elements of the administration of the property of others are explicitly referenced by the law, in sections 1400 et seq. of CC, as being subject to the regulations of the administration of the property of others. That is the case with the trust fund (section 1456 of CC), the administration of an associated foundation fund (section 351 of CC) and the administration of probate (section 1678 of CC). However, some other relations may likewise be governed by rules for the administration of the property of others as long as the general elements of the administration of the property of others are met and the nature of the specific relation does not exclude the application due to some other reason.

406. It cannot be ruled out that in some situations the rules for the administration of the property of others may be applied on the basis of analogy. That will concern mainly those cases where someone holds an ownership right to a specific thing but, at the same time, is obliged to handle it for the benefit of some other person or for some other purpose, e.g., in *the role of an agent for security,* who has been given some security for the benefit of creditors different from the agent himself or herself (section 2010 of CC).

407. Last but not least, the law also subsumes some legal relations within the rules for the administration of the property of others even *where no administration of the property of others is concerned.* This involves, among others, the regulation of the position of the creditor who has, for the purpose of security, been assigned an ownership right to a thing that is simultaneously handed over to him or her. The law subsumes the role of the creditor (in section 2042 of CC) under the rules of so-called simple (for more details, *see* below) administration of the property of others, regardless of the fact that the creditor is the owner of the thing during the decisive period of time. The law mentions, in connection with the administration of the foundation principal (‘*nadační jistina*’ in Czech; section 340 of CC), that the regulation for the administration of the property of others should be applied only in a reasonable manner and to a limited extent.

408. However, all of the situations above are mere exceptions to a rule. Thus, when the regulations for the administration of the property of others are applied to them, particular attention needs to be paid to the specific nature of such legal relations, and the regulations must be applied only in a subsidiary way – the manner and the extent of their application should not be in conflict with such legal relations.

III. Other Forms of Administration Not Subject to the General Regulation of Administration of Property of Others

409. While some situations may meet the elements of the administration of the property of others, they are *not subject to the application* of the general rules for the administration of the property of others. Those rules of ‘other administration’ then have a priority over the regulation of administration of the property of others as defined in sections 1400 et seq. of CC, typically entirely excluding their application to such cases (i.e., the administration of the property of others does not have the nature of a regulation that can be applied even in a subsidiary manner).

This concerns, above all, the regulation of *the role of members of bodies of legal persons.*

410. Although it might be generally argued that, when exercising their roles, such members perform a certain kind of administration of the property of others, the application of the rules for the administration of the property of others is ruled out by the special regulation of internal relations of legal persons. The same approach needs to be applied to the role of a liquidator of a legal person.

411. In addition, the rules for the administration of the property of others shall not be applied to the administration of assets represented by a guardian or a statutory representative (section 461 of CC) and in the regime of *the administration of the assets of a child* (section 896 of CC), where the law provides for a specific regulation in each case. Different is also the role of *a community of owners* (*'společenství vlastníků'* in Czech) when exercising the administration of a residential house (section 1194 of CC) and the role of a receiver in bankruptcy.

412. In some cases, the law *explicitly prohibits* the application of the rules for the administration of the property of others, namely in the entire extent (section 59, subsection 1 of ABC) or partially (section 195a, subsection 3 of Act on Capital Market Business;[271] section 5 subsection 3 of ICIF). However, it is evident that in all those provisions the existence of a special form of administration (or, as the case may be, the priority of a special regulation), may be deduced even without such a statutory explication.

IV. Inception of Administration of the Property of Others

413. The rules for the administration of the property of others shall (save for the above-stated exceptions) apply in *relation to all legal relations that functionally meet the elements of administration of the property of others*. Where the goal of such relations is the assignment of certain assets and their entrustment to an administrator to be administered for a certain purpose, the situation constitutes administration of the property of others. The inception and the termination of administration are then governed by such legal relations or, as the case may be, by the legal reason for their inception. The legal reason may arise on the basis of a contract or through some other means, e.g., due to the operation of law.

414. Administration of the property of others thus comes into existence where there are, on the one hand, *(relatively) independent assets, also referred to as a 'fund'*, and, on the other, a set *purpose* for which the fund is to be administered. The fund is constituted by a thing or a set of things entrusted to an administrator, who is to administer the same under certain conditions separately from the administrator's own property, as well as by any liabilities attached to such property or arising in connection with its administration.[272]

415. The assignment implies *exclusivity of administration*, i.e., the assets in the fund may be disposed of exclusively during the administration of the fund ('the administration is exclusive'). The existence of a fund is not conditioned by the change of the ownership of the things constituting the fund (i.e., property that is assigned in this manner may remain in the ownership of the person who entrusted it to the administrator), but the things constituting the fund must be certain. The identity of a fund is different from the individual things and liabilities that form it.

271. Act No. 256/2004 Sb.

272. Roy Goode & Ewan McKendrick, *Goode on Commercial Law* (London: Penguin Group, 4th edition, 2010), 65.

During the term of administration, the administrator may, thus, dispose of individual things or liabilities making up the fund, given any possible limitations, without such action impacting the existence of the fund. Where one thing is replaced with another, the fund is still constituted by the other thing. The same holds for debts. However, if all things in the fund are transferred without any consideration, or if all things making up the fund cease their existence, the existence of the fund likewise terminates. Logically, its administration then inevitably terminates as well.

416. The administration of the property of others must have a set *purpose*. The law anticipates that the purpose is set for the benefit of a specific person, who is then referred to as a '*beneficiary*' ('*beneficient*' in Czech, section 1400, subsection 1 of CC). The property of others may, however, also be administered for some other purpose, e.g., public enlightenment, support of sports or financing the construction of a church. There is no reason not to reasonably apply the rules for the administration of the property of others to funds that are being administered for such 'impersonal' purposes.

V. Termination of Administration of Property of Others

417. Where *the purpose of administration has been reached*, or the purpose terminates or is frustrated (as is the case when beneficiary's right to the administered property is terminated), *administration of the property of others terminates* because there is no further reason for its continuation. The administration may be established for a definite period of time (such a temporal limitation may also be understood as a certain aspect of the purpose of administration), and the passage of such a period of time likewise results in the termination of administration (cf. section 1439 of CC).

418. The termination of administration must be distinguished from *the termination of the exercise of one's performance of the role of an administrator* of the property of others. The moment of termination of the exercise of the role of an administrator may (but need not) coincide with the termination of existence of the administered fund. The identity of the fund need not be affected by the termination of the activity of one administrator. That is the case where the exercise of the function is entrusted to several administrators or where the administration of the fund is taken over by a new administrator.

419. The general rules for administration of the property of others found in the CC also regulate the termination of the exercise of the administrator's activity, which is linked to the administrator's resignation, revocation, limitation of legal capacity and certification of bankruptcy status (cf. sections 1438, 1440 and 1441 of CC). Those situations may also be regulated differently under the specific rules set for property administration.

420. Where the administration terminates, the administrator shall hand over the administered property (as long as there is some property to be handed over) under the rules of the administration to the beneficiary, unless provided otherwise. Where it is only the administrator's activity that terminates, with the fund to be further administered in the future, the administrator shall hand over the administered property to the new administrator (section 1446 CC).

VI. Administrator of the Property of Others

A. *Scope of Administrator's Activity, Types of Administration, Personal Nature of the Role of Administrator*

421. The rules for the administration of the property of others do not deal with the issue of specific legal relations governing the legal position of the administrator.[273] Nevertheless, they presume that the administrator of the property of others is essentially authorised (and simultaneously obliged) to exercise all rights to the administered property. However, this general scope of the administrator of the property of others is usually limited in specific cases.

The limitations may follow from the legal relation that constitutes the legal reason for administration, as well as from a specific regulation of administration of the property of others. The nature of the limitation of the administrator's scope of activity is also given by the purpose of the administration.

422. The purpose of administration may also be delimited with respect to the administered property. The law distinguishes between *a simple administration of the property of others*, whose purpose (whether final or only partial) is the preservation of the administered property (section 1405 of CC), and *a full administration of the property of others*, whose aim does not limit the administrator as to how to dispose of the property during the process of administration (section 1409 of CC).

423. The type of administration may arise from the conditions of a specific administration explicitly or in an implied manner. Thus, for instance, section 2042 of CC directly mentions the regime of simple administration. In other cases, however, the nature of the administration may be delimited in terms of subject matter – where the purpose of administration is defined exclusively as the preservation of the administered property, one deals with simple administration.

424. Simple administration limits the administrator's scope of activities with respect to the manner of disposing of the property administered as follows: the administrator may not change the purpose served by the administered property (section 1406 CC); the administrator may alienate or encumber the property only with the beneficiary's approval and subject to the conditions and extent necessary in the interest of preservation of its value, substance and purpose (section 1408 of CC). Where the administrator of the property of others invests any financial means while

273. Section 1400 subs. 2 of CC sets a rebuttable presumption, applicable only in cases of doubt about the administrator's role, that the administrator acts as a representative of the owner of the administered thing.

being in the regime of simple administration, he or she must do so with an increased level of care (section 1407 of CC). Where the administrator operating in the regime of simple administration violates such limitations, he or she acts ultra vires.

425. As regards the investment of financial means, the regime of simple administration is subject to limitations arising from the regulation of what is known as '*watchful investment*' ('*obezřetné investice*' in Czech; sections 1432–1436 of CC), forcing the administrator to adopt a conservative investment strategy. However, it needs to be mentioned that the cursory nature of this regulation raises some doubts about whether it can serve as a truly effective guidance to administrators.

426. Unlike simple administration, the administrator of the property of others who has been entrusted with *full administration* of the property of others should strive to increase the value of the administered property (rather than merely preserving it). This gives the administrator the right to do anything with the administered property that is necessary and useful (section 1410 of CC). In some cases, full administration arises directly from law; that is the case with the trustee with respect to the property in a trust fund (section 1456 of CC).

427. Regardless of the type of administration, the scope of the administrator's activities may be limited by the prohibition of some specific actions or the requirement *to have certain steps approved by other persons*. The latter may include the requirement of an approval by the beneficiary, the settlor, or some other persons assigned to carry out supervision or similar activities (e.g., in the role of the so-called protector in case of trust funds).

428. The statutory rules governing administration require the beneficiary's approval in many actions that may give rise to *a conflict of interest on the part of the administrator* (*see also* below). Where such approval cannot be obtained because the person is not known, or his or her approval cannot be obtained in time, or the person refuses to issue the approval without having a justified reason, then the person's approval may be replaced by the court (section 1404 of CC).[274]

429. The law further limits the scope of the administrator's activities in transferring, *free of charge,* the property that is being administered. Where the administrator transfers the administered property free of charge, this may involve only property of insignificant value and such a transfer must be in the beneficiary's interest, or serve the purpose of the administration in some other manner (section 1416 of CC). Any property of a higher than insignificant value may be transferred by the administrator only if such a need arises from the purpose of the administration (that will typically concern transfers for the benefit of beneficiaries of such administration arrangements).

274. Although s. 1404 of CC mentions on the beneficiary's approval, a more extensive interpretation is needed in our opinion, to reflect the functionally similar alternatives (that are more frequently found in legal practice).

430. Since there may be more than one administrator of a single fund constituting the administered property, the rules of the administration may require that the administrators act jointly. This requirement constitutes a limitation of the scope of the administrators' activity; any administrator acts ultra vires if he or she acts independently in such a situation.

431. The exercise of the role of an administrator of the property of others has *a personal nature.*[275] This means that the administrator may not fully delegate his or her decision-making (discretionary) powers to third persons (section 1401 of CC) with respect to disposing of the administered property. Where the administrator does so, he or she bears the same responsibility as if he or she were making the decision himself or herself.

432. However, it is not in conflict with the personal nature of the exercise of the role of the administrator of the property of others if the administrator delegates (either by means of direct or indirect representation or on the basis of some other obligation) his powers to a third person only for the purpose of a singular legal act, i.e., for the purpose of an act whose material content is determined by the administrator's decision. In such a case the administrator is liable only where he or she did not chose the third person with sufficient care or did not issue sufficient instructions to him or her.

433. Where the administrator of the property of others entrusts, for instance, a securities market broker with the escrow of a portfolio of securities, giving the instruction that the broker may dispose of the securities entrusted to him only on the basis of the administrator's instructions, then the administrator shall not be liable for the loss of the securities as long as he or she chose the broker carefully.

434. The rules of administration may *moderate* the personal nature of the exercise of the role and may allow *a broader range of possible delegations of powers*; the administrator, however, should never use this possibility to hold himself or herself not liable for the strategic management of administration and the obligation to supervise the exercise of any delegated activities.

B. Duties of Administrator of the Property of Others

435. The administrator of the property of others is obliged to exercise his or her role *with due diligence* (section 1411 of CC). While the concept of due diligence has a general character, its material delimitation can be found in the CC as part of the general regulation of bodies of legal persons (section 159, subsection 1 of CC). *Acting with due diligence means acting with all necessary loyalty, knowledge and care.* As a result, the administrator is obliged to administer the property entrusted in

275. Cf. a similar regulation in s. 159 subs. 2 of CC in relation to an elected member of a legal person but also in s. 438 of CC concerning representation and s. 2434 of CC concerning instruction. All those cases are basically fiduciary relations that have an essentially personal nature.

his or her care in the same manner as it would be administered by a duly diligent individual with all necessary knowledge for the benefit of another person towards whom he or she feels a moral obligation.[276] As it is *an objective standard*, it is irrelevant whether the administrator actually has the required knowledge or how he or she handles the management of his or her own affairs.

436. If the administrator discovers that he or she lacks the necessary knowledge, he or she must secure relevant advisors or resign to his post; the same applies where he or she is unable to meet the requirement of due diligence for any other reason. The requirement of loyalty reflects the fiduciary nature of the relationship. The regulation of the administration of the property of others further develops this requirement by specifying some additional obligations on the part of the administrator.

437. The administrator of the property of others must act in an honest and impartial way in the interest of all beneficiaries. The administrator may not prioritise the interests of a single beneficiary or a group of beneficiaries and put them before the interests of other beneficiaries, or his own in case the administrator is a beneficiary himself/herself (section 1412 of CC). This requirement must be taken into account even if the administrator directly or indirectly decides upon the distribution of profits and expenses incurred in connection with the administration (section 1403 of CC).

438. These 'active' duties are complemented with the administrator's 'negative' duty to avoid situations where his or her own interest could be in conflict with the interest of the administration or the beneficiaries. This duty has two components: the obligation *to inform* the beneficiaries or persons authorised with supervision over the exercise of the administration of any potential *conflict of one's interests* (section 1413 of CC) and (unless the rules for administration imply otherwise) the obligation not to perform, without the beneficiary's approval, any transactions that might place the administrator in a conflict of interests (section 1415 of CC). In this connection, let us note the existence of *the prohibition to use to one's own benefit*, without the beneficiary's approval, not only the administered *property* but also *any information* obtained during the administration.

439. The administrator must act *in a transparent way*. He or she is obliged to keep reliable records about the administered property and prevent any mixing of his or her own property and the property under administration (section 1414 of CC). Under the law, the administrator is also obliged to submit accounting records to the beneficiary at least once a year (section 1436 of CC) and upon the termination of administration (section 1445 of CC), and enable the beneficiary to inspect the accounting records and any other records related to the administration (section 1437 of CC).

276. This is inspired by the English judicial decision in *Whiteley v. Learoyd* case (1886) cit. in Gary Watt, *Trusts and Equity* (London: Oxford University Press, 3rd edition, 2008), 361.

440. The obligation of the administrator of the property of others *to compensate any harm* caused in connection with the administrator's breach of duty when administering the property is governed primarily by the legal relation that gives rise to the administration. The regulation of the administration of the property of others contains several special provisions whose practical meaning is limited (cf. sections 1416, 1417 and 1430 of CC).

441. What is interesting is the express authorisation of the administrator who administers the property of others free of charge, even if the matter is not addressed in the rules for administration in any way, to have himself or herself insured against property liability at the beneficiary's expense, or, as the case may be, at the expense of the property that is being administered (section 1427, subsection 2 of CC). Thus it holds, *a contrario*, that where the administrator is paid for performing the administration, then he or she (unless the rules of administration provide otherwise) bears any expenses for liability insurance at his or her own cost.

442. An important issue is the administrator's obligation in cases of a breach of the ban on transactions that involve the conflict of interest in the sense of section 1415 of CC (*see* above). Though the beneficiary may sue the administrator for compensation of any harm caused, it frequently will not be possible to find out about the breach at all.

443. Although the situation resembles cases of a breach of no-competition provisions of members of bodies of business corporations, the regulation of the administration of the property of others lacks an explicit rule, as in section 5 of ABC, forcing the administrator to surrender, for the benefit of the administered property, any benefit obtained as a result of such a breach. However, we believe that the same solution can be arrived at also in cases involving the breach of conflict of interest when administering the property of others, namely by applying the general regulation of unjust enrichment (section 2991 of CC).

444. Any act by an administrator of the property of others in breach of the ban on transactions potentially involving a conflict of interest is, without any doubt, an act without a just cause. Another conceptual feature of unjust enrichment, namely the enrichment 'at the expense of someone else' cannot be understood merely as a requirement that some harm be caused. Rather, it should be understood in a broader sense as a delimitation of some bond between the enriched party and the party suffering the loss.[277] This bond is, in this case, established due to the function of the statutory ban, which is the beneficiary's protection, i.e., the purpose of the administration of the property of others.

277. *See*, for instance Jan Petrov in Milan Hulmák et al., *Občanský zákoník VI. Závazkové právo. Komentář* (Praha: C. H. Beck, 2014), 1867.

VII. The Role of Third Persons

445. The CC contains a special regulation of the extent to which the administrator and the beneficiary are obliged towards third parties in cases of administration of the property of others (sections 1419–1422 CC). These provisions are important mainly because they are different from rules that otherwise generally govern legal relations that give rise to administration of the property of others (cf. section 436 of CC as regards representation and section 2456 of CC as regards consignment). That is because the law provides for them *in a mandatory manner* and they cannot be subject to any contractual deviation (cf. section 978 of CC).

446. The rules for the administration of the property of others offer a better protection to beneficiaries because, in substantial cases, they limit the satisfaction of claims arising in connection with the administration only to the property under administration (creditors thus cannot seek satisfaction from some other property of the beneficiary).

447. The law distinguishes two basic kinds of situations. The first concerns situations when the administrator acts within the limits of his or her powers and the second concerns cases of acting ultra vires. In the former case, the consequences of the administrator's acts with respect to third persons differ depending on whether it is evident, with respect to third persons, whether the administrator acts at the expense of the administered property or the beneficiary or not.

448. Where *it is evident* that the administrator acts within his or her powers as the administrator of the property of others, then *no personal obligation arises* to him or her from such an act. As a result, third parties may seek satisfaction of any claims only from the property administered or from the beneficiary (probably also from some other property than that is subject to administration). By contrast, where it is not evident that the administrator acts as an administrator of the property of others, the administrator assumes a personal obligation and third parties may seek compensation of their claims not only against the property administered but also against the administrator's own property. However, they may not seek any performance from the beneficiary beyond the property entrusted to the administrator.

449. Where the administrator acts ultra vires and *the third party was not in good faith*, the third party may seek satisfaction of their claims only against the personal property of the administrator (i.e., not against the property administered as well).

450. However, *if the third party was in good faith*, or where the beneficiary eventually approves such administrator's excessive act, then the third party may also seek satisfaction of their claims against the administered property. Similar to the above situation, third parties may not seek any performance from the beneficiary beyond the property entrusted to the administrator.

VIII. Trust Fund

A. Trust Fund: Characterisation, Legal Framework

451. *The trust fund* is a special instrument for the administration of property that has a multifaceted application (e.g., for the administration of family assets, joint investment or the settlement of property after divorce). It is an innovative normative construction that was introduced into the Czech legal system with the intention of enabling the formation of a legal construct comparable to the Anglo-American trust.

452. The regulation of *the trust fund contained in the CC* has been inspired by the concept of fiducia/trust in the QCC of 1994. As a result, a new instrument appeared in Czech law. This is an example of *a legal transplant* that is gradually finding its place into the legal system and testing its compatibility. The Québec regulation, however, was not taken over verbatim; legislators diverged from it in several respects. This fact needs to be taken into account when interpreting the individual provisions, mainly in relation to considerations on the transferability of arguments from foreign judicial decisions and legal doctrines (from Québec).

453. The same holds for using conclusions drawn in Anglo-American concepts of trust (originating in Great Britain and the US) because they are likewise different, as are other regimes of trusts and trust-like instruments. It will always be necessary to consider the overall context and teleological background of national and foreign regulations, which may lead to different conclusions. At the same time, however, one must honour the operating principles of trust structures, particularly as regards their differences from (business) corporations and other structures that may – at first sight – show some similarity. It is a matter of several decades before a body of judicial decisions and a legal doctrine are developed. The shape of the legal doctrine will depend on many diverse factors.

454. The legal framework of the trust fund is incorporated in sections 1448–1474 of the CC. This legal regulation is complemented with a regulation of the administration of the property of others (sections 1400–1447 of CC), which shall be applied in a subsidiary manner to trust funds (for more details on the nature of the administration of the property of others, *see* above).

455. Even though the regulation of administration of the property of others is included, following the model of the Québec regulation, in Part III on absolute property rights, no 'additional' right in rem is construed in the administration of the property of others. The mutual relations between the individual parties (settlor, trustee, beneficiary) have an obligatory nature.

The trust fund forms autonomous assets, i.e., property assigned for a particular purpose and liabilities (debts) related to its administration. A specific feature of the trust fund is that it represents *separated and independent ownership.* That means

respect to third persons) due to being identified as an apparent act (section 551 of CC) or a simulated legal act (section 555, subsection 2 of CC), or the transfer of property for the benefit of such a trust fund may be found as voidable (section 589 of CC). It may also be problematic if acknowledgement of such a structure is sought in some other country.

468. The trust fund may also be established for the purpose of entrepreneurial activity and investment for profits that are to be distributed between the settlor, employees, members or other persons. In this way, the trust fund differs from foundations (endowments and endowment funds), where any entrepreneurial (profit-making) purpose is ruled out. Some specific types of funds may include, among other, trust funds of collective investment (established only by investment companies under the ICIF) or securing trust funds (for the purpose of securing debts).

469. The law makes it possible for various types of trust funds to be established. They can serve, above all, for the effective administration of one's own or family property (including its protection), as a means of passing it over to the 'next' generation (as an alternative to inheritance), for ensuring the continuity of entrepreneurial activities, for tax optimisation, as a form of entrepreneurial activities (business trust fund), for the investment of assets (investment trust fund), as well as for securing the property (securing trust fund). When establishing a trust fund, the law distinguishes between three steps: creation – establishment – inception, with each of those steps being linked to a different legal fact and having different legal effects.

C. Creation of a Trust Fund, Charter, Name

470. A trust fund is created as a result of an expression of the settlor's will, whereby a certain part of the settlor's property is assigned ('separated' or 'made independent') for the performance of a particular purpose, and that part of the property is entrusted into the administration of a trustee. The law intentionally uses the expression 'creation' ('*vytvoření*' in Czech) in order to emphasise its difference from legal persons (foundation, establishment). A trust fund may be created during the life of the settlor (an *inter vivos* trust fund) or set up in case of the settlor's death (a *mortis causa* trust fund).

471. Following the Québec regulation, the CC is based on the concept that an *inter vivos* trust fund is created *on the basis of a contract*, which is typically concluded between the settlor and the trustee,[280] i.e., not only by means of a unilateral legal act of the settlor. The contractual basis is a residue of the Québec conception, or – more precisely – of French fiducias, which is strongly evident in trust funds. At

280. However, it is not impossible for the settlor to conclude a contract with, for instance, the beneficiary.

the same time, the trust fund differs from both Anglo-American trusts and foundations (with legal personality), which are, by contrast, established on the basis of a unilateral manifestation of the settlor's will (also where there are several settlors).

The contract typically contains not only the manifestation of the settlor's will, whereby a particular property is being assigned for a given purpose, but also the trustee's obligation to administer (in harmony with the settlor's will) the property thus assigned for the benefit of the beneficiary. The law does not require any specific form for the contract. However, if the property that is being assigned into the trust fund is constituted, for instance, by real estate, then the contract under which the real estate is being assigned into the trust fund must have a written form because the law requires the written form for any transfer of real estate.

472. A *mortis causa* trust fund may be created by a disposition in the event of a death, i.e., on the basis of a last will, a codicil or an inheritance contract. The disposition must contain all the elements of a charter ('*statut*'; section 1452, subsections 1 and 2 of CC) as well as meet the formal requirements placed on such dispositions by probate law in the event of a death. The trustee then exercises the rights of an heir or a legatee at the expense of the trust fund.

473. Apart from the creation, the establishment of a trust fund requires a charter (section 1452 of CC), which is a unilateral manifestation of the settlor's will having all the statutory formal elements (i.e., the necessity of being written up *in the form of a public deed*) as well as the required content.

474. This conception contains a clash between the classic approach to fiduciary relations in the continental European tradition of *ius commune* as a primarily contractual agreement on the one hand, and the conception of a trust (or foundation, as the case may be) on the other, which are being established on the basis of a unilateral legal act.

475. The statutory requirement for the trust fund charter to have the form of a public deed (a notarial deed) distances the trust fund (somewhat inappropriately) from classic trust structures, bringing it closer to investment funds or endowment funds. That not only causes some ambiguity concerning the meaning, sense and purpose of trust funds but also results in a somewhat unwelcome shift from an obligational sphere to a status sphere, which is even strengthened by the compulsory registration.

476. The (minimal) obligatory elements of the charter include the following (section 1452, subsection 2 of CC):

(a) the designation of the trust fund;
(b) the designation of the property constituting the trust fund at its inception;
(c) the delimitation of the purpose of the trust fund;
(d) the conditions for performance from the trust fund;
(e) information about the duration of the trust fund; where no information is given, the trust fund is understood to be established for an indefinite period of time;

(f) in the event that the trust fund should be used to give performance to a specific person as the beneficiary, the identification of such a person or the manner in which the beneficiary is to be identified; and
(g) the number of trustees and the manner in which they act.

477. The legislators have thus clearly conceived *the charter of the trust fund as its fundamental document*, which lays out the basic principles and rules of its operation. In this way (unlike the Québec model), it substantially reduces the importance of the contract that the trust fund gives rise to (section 1448, subsection 1 of CC).

478. However, that does not exclude the possibility that the charter itself delimits the said issues by relatively general rules (principles), while delegating their further specification to other persons as part of the administration of the trust fund, or authorising such persons (e.g., a group of protectors) to accept additional rules for the purpose of carrying out the provisions contained in the charter. The charter may (and regularly will) also contain many other rules according to which the property assigned to the trust fund will be eventually administered.

479. There is an obligatory requirement, in order to avoid interchangeability and deception, that the trust fund should bear *its own designation that is representative of its purpose*. A part of the designation must include the wording 'trust fund'. This is an obligatory element of the charter (section 1452, subsection 2(b) of CC).

480. Not all of the property needs to be given to the trust fund at its inception (cf. section 1468 of CC). The actual practice is quite the contrary: upon the inception of the trust fund, only a formal contribution is made, and the substantial amount of property is entrusted into the fund only after its inception.

481. The will manifested in the charter (or the contract) is binding upon not only the trustee and the beneficiary but also the settlor himself or herself (this is the so-called *duty of obedience*, particularly in relation to the set purpose). A question thus arises of whether *a later change of the charter* of the trust fund is possible or not.

482. If we take into consideration that the essence of the trust fund consists in the independence (separation) of the property assigned by the settlor, then it can be argued that the charter may be changed in those cases where the settlor expressly reserves, in the charter, the right of change and where the possibility is provided for by law (section 1469, subsection 2 of CC, by means of a court decision).

483. That is the fundamental difference between trust funds and foundations on the one hand and corporations on the other hand, where founders, members, partners and shareholders retain a substantial influence, having the power of even deciding upon the termination of the existence of the corporation. Should it be admitted that the change could be made at any time, then the intended separation of the property spheres would not be de facto made and the instrument would stop working (particularly as a tool for the protection of property).

484. Where the charter allows changes to be made, it does not automatically mean that any change is permissible. The individual changes must be primarily assessed from the point of view of section 1, subsection 2 of CC. For instance, the unlimited possibility of a change of the purpose could be found as incompatible with public order.

485. It must be realised that *the purpose of a trust fund constitutes the determining feature* of the independence of the property that makes up the trust fund. Should the purpose change, then a new trust fund is de facto being constituted, for which the law prescribes a specific procedure that is unlikely to be respected in such as case.

486. Thus, as long as it is at all permissible for the settlor to reserve to himself or herself or to some other person administering the trust fund the right to change the purpose of the trust fund, then the changes may only be such that they do not compromise the original purpose of the trust fund.[281] If the change of the charter of a trust fund interferes with the rights of third parties (the settlor or the beneficiaries), then it cannot be effective unless such persons express their approval with the change.

D. *Inception of a Trust Fund*

487. The so-called 'technical amendment' to the CC No. 460/2016 Sb. (effective from 1 January 2018) brought about a substantial conceptual change concerning *the inception of the trust fund.* The innovation is that the inception of the trust fund is tied to a constitutive entry in the registry of trust funds, kept under the Act No. 304/2013 Sb. on Public Registries of Legal and Natural Persons and Registry of Trust Funds.[282]

488. The constitutive entry does not concern only the trust fund but also beneficiaries in whose benefit the trust fund is being established. Without a record of the beneficiaries in the relevant registry, the beneficiary will not be able to seek his or her right to performance; that means that under that requirement, the law (somewhat illogically) deprives the beneficiary of the possibility of effective protection against unjustified detention of his or her benefit. At the same time, this requirement defies the raison d'etre for the very existence of the trust fund, namely to provide protection to beneficiaries from the abuse of the trustee's fiduciary position.[283]

281. *See* Vlastimil Pihera & Kateřina Ronovská, *Fundační principy a hranice jejich flexibility. K otázce možnosti dodatečných změn podmínek fungování svěřenských fondů a fundací* (Právník, Vol. 9/2018), 705.
282. *See* ss 65a et seq. of Public Register Act No. 304/2013 Coll.
283. For more details *see* Vlastimil Pihera, *Krocení trustů. Svěřenské fondy v hledáčku první novely občanského zákoníku* (Obchodněprávní revue, No. 5/2016).

489. To a certain extent, this approach defies the basic idea of the original legal construction, namely the creation of the trust fund on an obligational basis. The legislators have thus brought the legal regime of the trust fund closer to the regime of legal persons, including the duality of foundation/inception but refusing to give legal personality. That makes trust funds different from the comparable form of administration of the property in endowment funds (i.e., a legal entity with its own legal personality).

490. The *mortis causa* trust fund always comes into existence without any other conditions upon the death of the deceased/settlor (section 1451 of CC).

E. Establishment of a Trust Fund

491. Apart from creation and inception, the CC also provides for an establishment of a trust fund (*'zřízení svěřenského fondu'* in Czech), whereby a trustee of an *inter vivos* trust fund assumes his or her appointment for administration. The establishment of a trust fund is thus (in addition to its creation) another prerequisite for its inception. Where there are several trustees, it is enough for one of them to take over the appointment (section 1451 of CC).

492. With *mortis causa* trust funds, the trustee's non-acceptance of his or her appointment to administer the fund does not affect the inception of the trust fund. Unless the rules of the trust fund specify some other form of appointing the trustee, the trustee shall be appointed by court upon the motion of a person who has a legal interest in it (e.g., the beneficiary or the administrator of the property of the deceased). The relevant facts are then entered into the registry of trust funds only in a declaratory manner.

493. The moment the trustee accepts the administration of the property of the trust fund (upon inception or later), he or she is authorised to *full administration of the property* (*see* above about the duties of the administrator of the property of others). The trustee is then entered into public registries (such as the land registry) as the owner, with the additional note that this is a trustee so that it is clear to third persons that the property has been assigned into a trust fund.

F. Settlor of a Trust Fund

494. The settlor of a trust fund can be *an individual as well as a legal person*; there may also be several settlors. The settlor's position is unique and important not only during the creation of the trust fund but often also after its inception.

495. We agree with the approach that is traditionally acknowledged in case of trust and foundation structures abroad that the role of the settlor is principally tied to his or her person (i.e., it does not have a proprietary nature but a personal nature). As a result, *it cannot be assigned or inherited*, i.e., it terminates no later than upon the death of the settlor. The German legal doctrine refers to these rights as '*Gestaltungsrechte*'.[284] However, that does not mean that the settlor may not 'delegate' to other persons some of his or her rights that do not have an exclusively personal nature (e.g., the right to appoint a trustee or rights related to supervision over a trust fund).

496. Based on the stable doctrine and judicial decisions in other countries, such formative (personal) rights include the right to change the purpose of the structure, which is strongly and inseparably tied to the settlor. The same holds for the right of the settlor of foundations and institutions to withdraw/recall/cancel the same, as long as the law allows such a course of action.

497. The role of the settlor is also unique with view to the fact that even if someone increases the property of the trust fund after its inception, he or she does not become its settlor (for an express formulation *see also* section 1468 of CC).

498. Some rights are given to the settlor directly by the law, other rights may be reserved by the settlor in the charter or the contract, as the case may be.

The settlor has, above all, the following rights:

(a) To reserve the right to determine the beneficiaries even after the inception of the fund.
(b) To repeal and assign an administrator.
(c) To supervise the administration of the trust fund (having, above all, the right to information, the right to be submitted accounting records,[285] and possibly also the right to issue a prior approval with some specific legal acts).
(d) To file a motion with a court to issue an injunction forcing or banning the trustee to act in a certain way.[286]

499. The settlor may reserve in the charter for himself/herself or for other persons some possibility of intervention in the administration (including joint decision-making). However, the higher the degree of intervention reserved by the settlor, the higher the risk that doubts may arise about whether the trust fund has been really created as autonomous assets separated from the settlor's own property. An insufficient separation of the property spheres may have serious consequences (including the risk of the entire existence of the trust fund being challenged; the possibility of the initial manifestation of the settlor's will being found voidable; as well as consequences concerning bankruptcy and execution).

500. The settlor should likewise not have the possibility to give the trustee 'operational' instructions (or guidance) for acting in a certain way. That is because

284. On this topic *see* for instance the decision by the FLOGH of Liechtenstein of 29 Jan. 1990, LES 1991, 91 (106), and also Petr Lavický & Katerina Ronovská, *New Czech Foundation and Trust (Like) Law: Initial Experience and Reactions* (Trust and Trustees Vol. 6/2016), 641–646.
285. Cf. s. 1465, subs. 1 of CC.
286. Cf. s. 1466, subs. 1 of CC.

the trustee is obliged to exercise his or her role with due diligence, which would be disrupted by such a course of action. The trustee is also obliged to respect the interests of beneficiaries, which need not always be necessarily in harmony with the settlor's interests.

501. It is therefore common in practice for a settlor to manifest, when creating the trust fund, his or her will in the so-called *letter of wishes*, in order to indicate how the property is to be administered, and to set limits for how the property is to be used. Although the document does not typically have a legal force, it is very important because its content plays a key role in the administration of the property.

G. Beneficiary of a Trust Fund

502. The beneficiary ('obmyšlený/beneficient' in Czech) is a person for whose benefit the trust fund is being formed and for whose benefit the property that has been assigned in this manner is to be administered. The beneficiary may (but need not) be specified in concrete terms in the charter. Apart from that, the trust fund may be created for some other objectively delimited purpose that does not serve the benefit of a specific person.

503. The charter may also *merely delimit a category of persons*, out of which a beneficiary is to be chosen, in which case it is the trustee who identifies the beneficiary from such persons (given that other conditions mentioned in the charter are met). This situation constitutes a so-called *discretionary trust fund*, with the trustee being able to identify a beneficiary for each individual performance and even on repeated occasions.

504. There are some doubts about whether the settlor may establish a trust fund for the benefit of persons that he or she will only subsequently identify (that conclusion may be implied by the wording of section 1457, subsection 1 of CC). First of all, it needs to be stated that it is not possible to admit the existence of a trust fund lacking any determination of the category of future beneficiaries, leaving such a specification only up to the settlor's future free decision. Should that be the case, the trust fund would lack the set purpose, which forms a basic prerequisite for its inception.

505. By contrast, it might be accepted that the settlor has a limited possibility to modify the specification of the beneficiaries. However, such a right corresponds to the right of changing the purpose of the trust fund; for that reason, this issue is subject to the same argument as stated above about the change of the charter and the purpose of the trust fund. It is questionable whether the settlor may reserve the right to identify, after the inception of the trust fund, beneficiaries from the category of persons listed in the charter. We are, rather, of the opinion that such a procedure is not possible because the law vests this power in the trustee, while the settlor may not be the sole trustee (section 1454 of CC).

506. The beneficiary, if specified, has the right to be given performance by the trustee from the property in the trust fund under the conditions specified in the charter (as well as any other conditions in the charter). The performance may have the form of the right to receive payment of a certain amount, the right to proceeds, and even the right to the payment of the entire property under administration.

507. In trust funds with a private purpose, the beneficiary has the statutory (*ex lege*) right to performance under the conditions specified in the charter, but no later than hundred years after the creation of the fund. This rule is included in the act in the attempt to block the creation of trust funds without any temporal limitation (so-called *rule against perpetuity*).

508. The law directly assigns some rights to the beneficiary with respect to the trustee (section 1465 of CC). The beneficiary (as well as any other person who has the legal interest) may seek the nullification of the trustee's legal acts that harm the trust fund or the beneficiary's rights (section 1466 of CC).

There is a special relationship of obligation that exists between the trustee and the beneficiary in a sui generis fashion (it is not a contractual relationship). Its character approximates to that of the position of a beneficiary in contracts for the benefit of a third person;[287] the beneficiary therefore does not enjoy the right in rem to the property in the trust fund.

H. Trustee

509. The trustee is a person who administers the property assigned by the settlor into a trust fund. The trustee enjoys the full administration of the trust fund (section 1456 of CC). He or she therefore holds the position of an administrator of the property of others, and has the corresponding rights and obligations. For more details, see the discussion on the obligations of administrators of the property of others at the beginning of this chapter.

510. The trustee may *only be an individual with a full legal capacity or, as long as the law requires, a legal person.* Up until now, the authorisation to administer trust funds has been given only to some investment companies.[288]

511. The trustee may also be *the settlor or the beneficiary*. In that case, however, the trust fund must have another trustee who is a third person, and the two trustees may only act jointly (section 1454 of CC). Because this possibility is not common in the Anglo-American tradition, there is a risk that a trust fund set up in this manner may not be honoured abroad.

512. The legal position of the trustee (the trustee's rights and obligations) are determined mainly by the special regulation (sections 1448 et seq. of CC) and, in a

287. *See* Rainer Becker, *Die fiducie von Québec und der trust* (Tübingen: Mohr Siebeck, 2007), 237.
288. Cf. s. 11, subs. 6 of ICIF.

subsidiary manner, also the general regulation of the administration of the property of others (sections 1400 et seq. of CC). Other rules may be contained in the charter or the contract under which the fund is being created.

513. The trustee has the following powers:

(a) the right to hold and administer the assigned property (the trustee enjoys the full administration of property in the trust fund) with due diligence;
(b) the right to exercise ownership rights to the property in the trustee's own name at the expense of the fund (section 1448, subsection 3 of the CC);
(c) the duty to inform the beneficiary of the existence of the trust fund and enable him or her to inspect records, submit accounts, reports and information (section 1465, subsection 2 of CC);
(d) the right to appoint the beneficiary and determine the performance for the beneficiary, unless the settlor had done so and did not foresee some other solution (section 1457, subsection 2 of CC);
(e) the duty to bear a supervision of the trustee's activities; the supervision is carried out primarily by the settlor (or some other person identified in the charter), the beneficiary and, in certain cases specified by law, also the court upon a motion filed by a person who has a legal interest in the matter.[289]

514. It is the task of the trustee to increase the property and assert the beneficiary's interests (section 1409 of CC). The trustee may likewise do anything that is necessary and useful. The trustee is relatively free (unless there is some limitation in the charter or the contract) to alienate the property for monetary consideration (section 1408 of CC *a contrario*), encumber the same (section 1408 of CC *a contrario*), invest it, etc. However, the trustee is always obliged to act with due diligence, which in itself implies a number of limitations.

515. The charter or the contract may provide for a different standard of administration: a more conservative simple approach to administration, or a combination of a simple and full approach. The question remains, however, what effects such a limitation may have towards third persons. It may be assumed that if the trustee oversteps the limits (acting ultra vires), the consequence would be a personal liability of the trustee towards third persons from such legal acts (section 1420 of CC).

516. Where the property assigned into a trust fund is subject to public legal registration (that typically concerns real estate and its registration in the Land Registry, but also vehicles, ships, aircraft, etc.), the trustee is entered into such registries with the note that the individual is a 'trustee' (section 1456 of CC).

517. The trustee is appointed and recalled by the settlor. However, the settlor may also determine some other form of appointment of the trustee, e.g., identify a third person authorised to perform the appointment. The existence of the role is also

289. In cases stipulated by law, the administration of the trust fund is also supervised by another person or group of persons or by a public authority.

conditioned by the trustee's acceptance of the appointment. Where the authorised person fails to appoint the trustee within a reasonable period of time, a person having a legal interest in the matter (typically the beneficiary) may file a motion with a court to appoint the trustee. The court shall proceed according the relevant procedural regulations (sections 93 et seq. of SJP).

518. Since the law does not specify any limitations concerning the recall of the trustee, it may be assumed that the settlor may recall the trustee even without any reason. This concept (while being different from the Québec model) implies a high degree of dependence of the trustee on the settlor, which may be undesirable in many respects. Where the charter of the trust fund does not rule this possibility out, such an authorisation by the settlor may lead to the conclusion that the settlor is still de facto in control of the trust fund, and, consequently, the trust fund is not constituted by independent property.

519. However, the law regulates the situation when the trustee cannot be appointed by the settlor. In that case, the appointment can be made by court (section 1455, subsection 2 of CC). A similar provision exists for the recall of a trustee (section 1466, subsection 1 of CC).

Unless the contract on the creation of a trust fund or the charter provide otherwise, the exercise of the activity of the trustee is subject to remuneration: the trustee is eligible for a usual remuneration (section 1402, subsection 1 of CC).

I. Supervision over a Trust Fund

520. The supervision over a trust fund is primarily the duty of the settlor and the beneficiaries; in exceptional cases, the supervision is carried out by the court, which also may, under conditions stipulated by law, even cancel the trust fund. Following the model of standard trust structures found abroad, it is common practice to establish the role of *the protector, or a group of protectors,* to carry out supervision over the administration of a trust fund. The protector performs the role of an internal body of supervision (it is similar to 'supervisory boards').

521. The reason for the existence of supervision over trust funds is, above all, *the preservation of the property for the purpose set by the settlor and the promotion of the settlor's will,* as well as supervision over the trustee's performance of the administration, the preservation of legal certainty and the protection of the rights of third persons (beneficiaries, creditors). The public interest in the preservation of property for the performance of the purpose set by the settlor is realised particularly in case of publically beneficial trust funds.

522. As regards trust funds with a private purpose, there are certain control mechanisms contained in the charter that serve the settlor and the beneficiaries. Public supervision over such structures is not so significant because these trust funds often deal with property relations for a limited group of people (e.g., family members), do not have a major economic impact, do not enjoy tax benefits, etc.

523. In matters of the trust fund, the court may decide upon the motion of a person authorised to file a motion within uncontested proceedings in matters of trust funds (sections 94–97 of SJP). In connection with the administration of property of trust funds, the possibility of court supervision also has motivational and preventive functions. It also has an ancillary function in those cases where the settlor has failed to establish any other mechanism of supervision in his or her manifestation of will (in the charter or the contract).

524. The court may adopt various measures, such as:

(a) to appoint persons authorised to supervise the administration of the trust fund in the interest of a not yet existing or unborn beneficiary (section 1464 of CC);
(b) to appoint the trustee of a trust fund;
(c) to make the trustee act or to ban the trustee from acting in a certain way, as well as to recall the trustee and appoint a new one (section 1466, subsection 1 of CC);
(d) to commit the settlor, beneficiary or some other person having a legal interest in the matter to file a motion for the commencement of proceedings or to lead the proceedings instead of a trustee who is inactive without a sufficient reason (section 1466, subsection 2 of CC);
(e) to cancel the trust fund or to replace the original publically beneficial purpose with some other similar purpose (section 1469, subsection 1 of CC);
(f) to modify the charter of the trust fund (section 1469, subsection 2 of CC) – to transfer the property from a trust fund with a publically beneficial purpose to another trust fund or to the ownership of a legal person, while making sure the purpose is as close to the original purpose as possible (section 1473 of CC).

J. Termination of Administration and Cessation of Existence of a Trust Fund

525. The administration of a trust fund terminates upon the occurrence of legal facts specified by law (passage of time, attainment of the purpose for which it was set, a judicial decision; cf. section 1471 of CC). Other facts may be anticipated in the charter or the contract (e.g., the meeting of some particular condition). Some other situations that give rise to the termination of existence of a trust fund are also possible, e.g., the exhaustion of all property. The administration of trust funds with a private purpose shall also end (unless the charter excludes the possibility) when all beneficiaries waive their right to performance from the trust fund (section 1471 of CC).

526. The duration of a trust fund may be determined in the charter by the settlor. However, the duration is limited by the maximum period of time in case of trust funds with a private purpose (in the sense of section 1460 of CC).

Where the purpose of the trust fund is 'unattainable', this does not automatically result in the termination of its administration. Rather, the procedure specified in section 1469 of CC is possible, namely a decision by the court on the cancellation of the fund in case the attainment of the purpose is impossible or difficult due to circumstances unknown or unforeseeable to the settlor. In case of publicly beneficial purposes, the law prefers the replacement of the original purpose with a similar purpose.[290]

527. Once the administration of a trust fund is terminated, the trustee shall not continue with the administration of the trust fund. Instead, he or she will dispose of the property assigned into the trust fund in harmony with section 1474 of CC, namely according to the charter, or may surrender it to the last entitled person (or entitled persons) in the sense of section 1472 of CC. The last entitled person has, as opposed to the beneficiary, a specific position because he or she enjoys a residual right sui generis.

528. Where all the property constituting the trust fund is handed over after the termination of the administration of the trust fund, *the trust fund shall cease its existence*. The handing over of all property from the trust fund is possible only after all debts encumbering the property in the trust fund are settled. The trustee is obliged to submit accounting records to the entitled person in the sense of section 1445 of CC.

529. The cessation of existence of a trust fund occurs only upon the transfer of the last 'remaining property', which is done on the basis of a contract concluded between the trustee and the last entitled person. The last entitled person may waive his or her right; in that case the remaining property passes to the state.

K. Comparable Legal Constructions for Administration of Property of Others

530. The CC offers several traditional (though innovated) instruments for the administration of property. In the field of foundation law, the CC contains a new regulation enabling property to be entrusted to a foundation, apart from foundations and endowment funds, in the form of an affiliated fund (*'přidružený fond'* in Czech; sections 349 et seq. of CC). All those forms of administering property share the existence of an assigned, or 'separated', property for a particular purpose and all have a fiduciary nature, i.e., the relationship of trust between the person who assigns the property and the person called upon to administer it.[291]

531. When choosing a suitable form of administration of property, there is *always a whole range of aspects* (legal as well as non-legal) to be taken into

290. The important difference here is also the extent of the publication duties in the public registry/the registry of trust funds.

291. For more details, *see* Bohumil Havel & Kateřina Ronovská in Luboš Tichý, Kateřina Ronovská & Miloš Kocí, *Trust a srovnatelné instituty v Evropě* (Praha: CPK, 2014), 141 et seq.

account, such as the flexibility of the legal regulation, the purpose, the group of beneficiaries, the limits for disposing of the property, the cancellability of a given structure. An important role is also played by *public law*, mainly requirements placed on the transparency of the structure chosen, as well as the tax regime.[292]

532. The fundamental difference between trust funds and foundations (and, especially, endowment funds) consists in the legal personality of foundations on the one hand and the sole obligation/right-in-rem nature of trust funds on the other. Other differences include the creation of *inter vivos* trust funds by means of a contract (as opposed to the unilateral manifestation of will in case of foundations), the delimitation of purpose (the purpose of a trust fund is broader), and the different requirements concerning the publication of information about settlors and beneficiaries.

L. Trust Funds and Procedural Law (1st Detour)

533. The regulation of civil court procedure respects the private law construction of the trust fund: it gives the fund neither the capacity to be a participant in civil court proceedings (section 19 of the CPC) nor any procedural competence. As a result, the trustee serves as the participant in all proceedings, acting either as the petitioner or the respondent in contested proceedings, or as a participant in uncontested proceedings concerning the trust fund. The trustee must be identified as a participant not only in the action but also in any remedial means, in the proposal for the enforcement of judgment, and in the proposal for the ordering of an execution.

534. In case of *contested proceedings*, the above-stated conclusion is indirectly confirmed by the regulation of how the trustee should be designated in the motion for the commencement of proceedings (section 79, subsection 1 of the CPC). In case of *uncontested proceedings*, an express delimitation of participants is specified in section 95 of SJP. The fact that the trustee acts not in his own matter but *at the account of the trust fund* is reflected in the manner in which the trustee is designated in the proceedings. Hence, in proceedings that concern the trust fund, the trustee is not only a participant to the proceedings but also performs all procedural acts. The local jurisdiction is governed by the seat of the general court of the trustee.

535. *Uncontested proceedings in matters relating to trust funds* are regulated in sections 94–97 of SJP; such proceedings may be started exclusively upon a motion.[293] The parties that are authorised to file the motion follow from those provisions of the CC that give the court the power to decide on certain issues pertaining to trust funds. The participants in the proceedings include the petitioner and those parties that the law specifies as participants (section 6, subsection 2 of SJP). In addition to the petitioner, the participants in matters involving trust funds include,

292. Katerina Ronovská & Petr Lavický, *New Czech Foundation and Trust (Like) Law: Initial Experience and Reactions* (Trust and Trustees Vol. 6/2016), 641–646.

293. Section 96 of SJP.

under section 95 of SJP, the settlor, the trustee, the beneficiary and the person authorised to supervise the administration of the trust fund (section 1463 of CC).

536. In proceedings to enforce a judgment (execution proceedings), the entitled party/obligor is, likewise, the trustee acting on behalf of the trust fund. Where the trustee appears in the proceedings because he or she acts on behalf of the trust fund, his or her own property sphere cannot be principally affected (as the obliged party). The execution may, in such a case, be led at the expense/to the benefit of the trust fund, which should also be evident from the way the trustee is identified in the judgment.

537. The nature of the trust fund as independent assets is also reflected *in bankruptcy law*. Bankruptcy is accorded independently in relation to a trust fund. Where the trustee of a trust fund is unable to cover, from the property in the trust fund, the financial debts incurred in connection with its administration, the state of insolvency may result. Where the trust fund operates a works, the trust fund may end up being overburdened with debts.

538. In insolvency proceedings, the trustee acts as the debtor within the extent to which he or she performs the administration of the trust fund. The property estate (assets) is constituted by the property within the trust fund. In insolvency proceedings, only those creditors who seek their satisfaction from the property of the fund may seek their claims.

The certification of the trustee's personal bankruptcy (i.e., in relation to his or her own personal property) is not applicable in case of a trust fund; such a situation, however, results in the termination of the position of the trustee (section 1438 of CC).

M. Accounting and Tax Regimes of a Trust Fund (2nd Detour)

539. Although a trust fund is not endowed with legal personality, it is considered by tax legal regulations as *a tax subject*, whose obligations are performed by the trustee. The trustee has the same rights and obligations as any other tax subject.[294] All trust funds have the same local jurisdiction of the tax administrator – the Internal Revenue Office for the Capital City of Prague, Territorial Division for Prague 7. The trust fund is always a taxpayer of income tax of legal persons, and, where applicable, also the tax on real estate, the tax on acquisition of real estate in case of an acquisition of a real estate against consideration, value added tax, if it performs economic activity, also advance payments for income tax from employment, withholding tax, etc. The trust fund is considered as a person for the purpose of most treaties on the prevention of double taxation.

294. A similar position is held, for instance, an administrator of a deceased person's property or a bankruptcy trustee.

540. As the trust fund is an accounting unit,[295] it is obliged to keep double entry bookkeeping on the accrual principle and compile accounting sheets according to Czech accounting regulations. Where it constitutes a larger accounting unit than a micro accounting unit, then its closing accounts must be verified by an auditor.[296]

541. The assignment of the property into the trust fund or the increase of the fund's property by contract or disposition in the event of death are considered, for the purpose of income tax, as contributions into a business corporation.[297] The proceeds of a trust fund are included in the tax base of the trust fund. The profit after taxation that is paid out to the beneficiaries is subject to a withholding tax in the amount of 15%. The payment of the property from the trust fund is included in the relevant income tax base of the beneficiary, unless such payment is tax exempt, as it is with the relatives of the person who contributed the property into the fund in the direct line and the enumerated persons in an indirect line, and other persons including those who transferred their property into the fund free of charge. For the purpose of exemption of income tax of legal persons on shares in profit and the profits from the sale of shares in business companies, the trust fund is considered as the mother company.[298]

295. Section 1, subs. 2 of the Accounting Act No. č. 563/1991 Coll.
296. Sections 1f and 20 of the Accounting Act No. č. 563/1991 Coll.
297. A similar tax regime concerns the contribution and the assignment (separation) of property into foundations or institutions.
298. The tax exemption shall be applied according to s. 19 of the Income Tax Act No. 586/1992 Coll.

Chapter 2. Security. *Fiducia cum Creditore* (*See Also* Parts I, II and V)

§1. Transfer of a Right (of Ownership) (in Real Property) as Security

542. Transfer of a right of ownership as security is regulated in the context of a general institution of transfer of a right as security in sections 2040–2044 of the CC.

Transfer of a right of ownership (in real property) as security is its *temporary transfer* to the creditor in order to secure discharge of a debt by the property owner (or a third party). It is an obligational instrument established by a contract in writing; however, the actual (temporary) transfer of a right of ownership in real property only takes place upon registration in the Land Register, whereby it also becomes a right in rem.

543. For years, this concept of security was suppressed by restrictions of fiduciary transfers as security, which were interpreted as prohibited lapsible pledged property.[299] However, the CC has overcome this and allows temporary transfers with resolutive and suspensive conditions.[300] The, however, presumes that unless stipulated otherwise, a transfer of right as security is a transfer with a resolutive condition that the debt will be discharged. In other words, a temporary transfer may be set up in a way that the debtor's right of ownership will be restored automatically after debt discharge, or that the creditor will have to transfer the right of ownership back by an active act. A transfer of a right of ownership as security is, therefore, extinguished upon satisfaction of the debt automatically or upon satisfaction of the debt together with an active act of the creditor.

544. A different situation occurs if a debt is not discharged and the transfer as security is to be executed. The law presumes that if a secured debt has not been discharged, the transfer of right as security becomes unconditional and the debtor will hand over to the creditor everything which is necessary for the full exercise of the transferred right. In other words, if there is no other agreement, the creditor becomes the owner of the real property and the information about the temporary character of the transfer will be deleted from the Land Register – the debtor is obliged to provide assistance to that end.

545. It is, however, common that the value of the security, i.e., the subject of the transfer of right as security, exceeds the amount of the secured debt. In this case, the law stipulates that the creditor will pay the person who provided the security an amount equal to the difference; in doing so, the creditor will include the costs reasonably incurred in connection with the exercise of the transfer of right as security. If the contract for the transfer of right as security does not specify the amount of debt and a reliable valuation of the right transferred as security, the creditor is required to prove that the usual value of the security evidently does not exceed the

299. Cf. especially Supreme Court Case No. 31 Odo 495/2006.
300. Cf. Petr Tégl, *Ještě k některým aspektům zajišťovacího převodu práva* (Obchodněprávní revue Vol. 8/2011), 223 et seq.

amount of the secured debt. On the contrary, if the amount of the debt exceeds the value of the security, the debtor must pay the difference.

546. The legal regulation only addresses the basic issues and, moreover, is dispositive. Therefore, details of this method of security are usually provided for by the actual contract on its establishment.

547. If the debtor becomes bankrupt in during the existence of the security, i.e., insolvency proceedings are initiated, the creditor secured by the transfer of the right of ownership in the real property is a secured creditor. However, he must file his claim in the insolvency proceedings, and the security will be realised in those proceedings.

548. The law does not prevent transfer to the creditor of another right as security associated with the real property but the transfer as security of a claim will usually take place in the regime of tangible property (*see* below Chapter 2, §4).

§2. Deviation from Transfer of a Right of Ownership (in Real Property) as Security

549. Similarly to pledge, transfer of a right of ownership in movable property as security is subject to what was set out above in Chapter 1, §3; however, the creation of that right is usually associated with the contract becoming effective. Where a right of ownership is subject to registration in the respective registry, any transfer of the right of ownership as security will also be registered in it (aviation registry, trademark registry, etc.).

Part V. Security

Chapter 1. Securities in Immovable Property

§1. PRIVILEGES

550. Every entity with a legal personality exhibits autonomy in terms of property and under the law of delicts,[301] that is, is liable for the fulfilment of its obligations with all its assets and unless provided otherwise by agreement or by law, this is a pro rata liability. Important aspects in determining the order of satisfaction of creditors include, in particular, the seniority of their claims; however, Czech law also enables parties to stipulate specific preferential rights. In addition to stipulating a security, which is usually the best instrument to strengthen the position of a particular creditor, it is also possible to stipulate other variants of preference – a subordination agreement, an agreement to change the order of reinsurance, retention of title, debt corroboration, etc. Some preferential rights arise from law (statutory partial subordination of associates in insolvency proceedings, priority of claims against the estate in insolvency proceedings, priority of in rem security over obligational security (section 1371(3) of the CC), etc.).

551. Current Czech private law contains standard forms of security as known in the Central European legal culture. The purpose of security is to strengthen the position of the creditor. At the same time, security has a compensatory function as it gives creditors sufficient resources for satisfaction. An important role is played by security instruments in insolvency law because secured creditors have a special position and rules for satisfaction (priority and *pari passu*). Therefore, security has an important *ex ante* function as creditors use it to ensure an improved position over other creditors in case of any future failure of the debtor.

552. Security can be stipulated as a right in rem or only in the regime of an obligation (suretyship, bank guarantee, etc.). In rem security is safer as it adheres to the property itself; however, it is more costly to establish and maintain. In contrast, obligational security is easier to establish but it typically does not establish a position of a secured creditor in insolvency proceedings. Security may be, with the creditor's consent, provided by the debtor or a third party.

301. Cf, e.g., Bohumil Havel in Filip Melzer & Petr Tégl et al., *Občanský zákoník. Velký komentář. Volume 1* (Prague: Leges, 2013) – commentary on s. 20(1).

553. In addition to security, Czech law also provides for debt corroboration, which, however, does not provide the benefits of security or any new property value; it only strengthens the legal position of a debtor (contractual penalty, acknowledgement of debt).

554. Since the trade world is variable, Czech law also offers various forms of quasi-security or specifically instruments that can to some extent also perform a security function – these typically include bill, retention of title or prohibition of alienation or securing of property.

555. In the Czech market standard, common concepts of syndicated (club) loans are used after 1989.[302] The CC stipulates in this respect an explicit possibility of establishment, administration and maintenance of security via an administrator of security (agent), and in this case, security is provided for the benefit of a group of creditors but it is performed by the administrator without that person having or having to have a claim from the debtor (section 2010(2) of the CC).

§2. Pledge (Mortgage)

I. The Nature, Function and Principles of Pledge (Mortgage)

556. A pledge is a security legal instrument providing the creditor with a material guarantee of fulfilment of a secured claim (security function) because the claim can be satisfied from the pledged property if the claim is not discharged properly and timely (compensatory function); the pledged property, however, does not become the creditor's property. At the same time, pledge provides the creditor with a priority position for satisfaction in collective insolvency proceedings.

557. Pledge is a right in rem (property right) of a pledgee to property of another; it operates not only between the parties to the pledge relationship but also vis-à-vis other acquirers of pledged property. Pledge restricts the exercise of the pledgor's rights of ownership in the pledged property especially by obliging him to tolerate the realisation of the pledged property to satisfy the secured claim.

558. A pledge is based on the following principles: *Accessory nature.* A pledge is only used to secure a claim, it does not have any other economic purpose. Its duration, therefore, depends on the existence of the secured claim. *Subsidiarity.* Satisfaction of the pledgee from the pledged property only comes into consideration when the secured claim is not discharged properly and timely. *Special character* (individualisation) of a pledge. In principle, a pledge may encumber only an individually determined property, including collective property.

302. Cf. Tomáš Richter, *Insolvenční právo* (Prague: Wolters Kluwer, 2nd edition, 2017), 285 et seq.

559. Pledge is regulated in the CC in Book Three Title Two Chapter Five providing for rights in rem in property of another, specifically in sections 1309 through 1394 of the CC – of course, also other provisions regulating general security apply.

II. Elements of a Pledge Relationship

560. When defining the entities, it is necessary to distinguish between an obligational relationship, which relates to a secured claim, and a pledge relationship, which applies to the regime of a pledge.

In an obligational relationship, one party is an *obligee*, who has a claim from the obligor, and the other party is an *obligor*, who is to settle the debt he owes to the obligee. This obligor's debt is secured by a pledge. In a relationship resulting from a pledge, one party is a *pledgee*, a person for whose benefit the pledge has been established; the pledgee is at the same time an obligee. The other party is a *pledgor*, who is always the owner of the pledged property. The obligor may be identical with the pledgor. In addition to this basic triad of entities, it is sometimes necessary to distinguish a pledgor and a *contracting pledgor* in pledge relationships; a contracting pledgor is a person who has pledged the property and is not an obligor.

561. A pledge may secure a pecuniary as well as a non-pecuniary claim; security of a pecuniary claim is more frequent in practice. A *pecuniary claim* must be individualised; its amount may be variable but it must be possible to determine its amount during the existence of the pledge. Unless agreed otherwise, a pledge relates to the entire claim including its accessories, and it also covers the cost of satisfaction from the pledged property.

562. A secured *non-pecuniary claim* may be, for example, a right for rendition of property or a right for creation of a work. In the case of non-pecuniary claims, a rebuttable presumption applies that the creditor is entitled to a payment not exceeding the amount of the usual price of the claim at the time the pledge was created. A pledge may also secure a conditional, future or time-barred claim.[303] Several claims may be secured by a pledge for the benefit of one obligee. These must be claims of a certain kind and at the same time arisen at a certain time, or different claims but arisen from the same legal cause.

563. *Pledged property* is a property value (a thing) that may be subject to a pledge. Where the pledged property is real estate, this is referred to as a mortgage. Pledged property must be transferable because satisfaction from the pledged property usually takes place through its realisation, i.e., a transfer of the right of ownership in the pledged property to another person.

It is also possible to pledge several things simultaneously – *simultaneous pledge*. The essence of simultaneous pledge is that the pledgee may be satisfied from any pledged thing or from all the pledged things.

303. Cf. Jan Krčmář, *Právo občanské. II. Věcná práva* (Prague: Všehrd, 1934), 303.

564. If pledged property is *divided* during the existence of a pledge, the pledge will encumber all the newly created things as a simultaneous pledge.[304] If pledged property is *transformed* into new property, the pledge will encumber this new property. If pledged property is merged with other property, the pledgee may seek restoration of the previous state at the expense of the pledgor; if this is not possible, the pledge will encumber the newly created property up to the value of the pledged property at the time of the merger.

565. It is possible to pledge not only property already existing and at the same time belonging to the same pledgor but also property in which the pledgor will acquire a right of ownership only in the future or which will only be created in the future (*future pledge*). In this case, conclusion of a contract only establishes a pledge, and the pledge is actually created upon acquisition of the right of ownership in the pledged property by the pledgor.

566. During the existence of a pledge, the right of ownership in the pledged property may be transferred (e.g., sale or donation) or may pass (e.g., inheritance, escheat, fall of hammer in an auction, expropriation). In such cases, a rule applies generally that neither transfer nor passage of the right of ownership affects the existence of the pledge; therefore, the acquirer of the pledged property becomes a pledgor.

567. The CC allows replacement of a secured claim during the existence of a mortgage (*replacement of a pledge*). This consists in the fact that the pledgor stipulates another pledge in an already encumbered property registered in a public register and at the same time seeks that a pledge established later is registered in the order of another, previously registered, pledge in the same property.

568. After an existing pledge registered in the Land Register is extinguished and has not yet been deleted from the Land Register, the CC also allows merger of that right, at that time existing only in the books (*released pledge*), with another pledge. In addition to the precondition of existence of registration of the original pledge in the Land Register, there is also a precondition that the subject of pledge still exists and that the newly secured claim does not exceed the originally secured one.

Both these instruments may be contractually excluded.

III. Existence of a Pledge (Mortgage)

569. A prerequisite for the creation of a pledge is a claim that may be secured by a pledge, eligible real property that will be pledged, and circumstances foreseen by the law associated with the creation of a pledge. The legal cause (*titulus*) for the

304. Cf. Supreme Court Case No. 29 Odo 661/2206 (Rc 105/2008) and Czechoslovak Supreme Court Case No. R II 411/35 (Vážný 14 549).

establishment of a pledge may be a pledge agreement, a decision of a public authority (court or an administrative authority), another legal fact stipulated by law (e.g., a testament), and law.

570. Another prerequisite for the creation of a pledge in the case of real property is the existence of another fact (*modus*),[305] that is, an entry in a public register (Land Register). A pledge of immovable property which is not subject to registration in a public register is created upon registration in the pledge registry, where this fact is recorded by a notary.

571. A *pledge contract* is a legal act that must, in addition to general elements, always define the pledged property and secured claims. Pledge contracts are subject to contractual autonomy but the CC prohibits arrangements stipulating that the pledgor or a contracting pledgor may not redeem the pledged property. It also prohibits to stipulate that until a claim becomes due, the pledgee will not claim satisfaction from the pledged property, that the pledgee may sell the pledged property in any manner or keep it for a price of his choice (referred to as lapsible pledged property), or that the pledgee may take fruits or revenues of the pledged property (prohibition of antichresis). Where the pledged property is real property, the pledge contract must always be in writing.

572. A pledge may be created by a *decision of a court or an administrative authority* only in cases expressly foreseen by law (e.g., establishment of a judicial or private enforcement pledge in the enforcement of a decision or a private enforcement, or establishment of a pledge by a tax administrator to secure an outstanding tax).

A pledge may exceptionally be created directly *by law* (e.g., under a usufructuary lease or forwarding agreement).

573. Czech law also provides for *negative pledge*,[306] that is, a possibility to stipulate that certain property will not be encumbered by a pledge. Such an arrangement primarily has effects only *inter partes*. However, where such prohibition is registered in a public register, it is effective *erga omnes*; if it is known to a particular person, it is effective against that person.

IV. Content and Realisation of a Pledge (Mortgage)

574. The rights and obligations of parties change depending on whether the secured claim has not yet become due (securing phase) or whether it is due (realisation phase).

305. For the dogma distinguishing *titulus* and *modus* cf. Jan Krčmář, *Právo občanské. II. Věcná práva* (Prague: Všehrd, 1934), 5–6.

306. Cf. Milan Hulmák in Milan Hulmák, Jan Petrov & Petr Lavický et al., *Občanský zákoník V. Závazkové právo. Obecná část (§ 1721–2054).* (Prague: C. H. Beck, 1st edition, 2014), 200 et seq.

In the *securing phase*, the pledgor may dispose of the property, i.e., use it, enjoy it, and legally dispose of it. However, the pledgor is obliged to refrain anything which cases the pledged property to deteriorate to the detriment of the pledgee. If the pledgor causes that the pledged property becomes insufficient as a result of the pledgor's acts, he is obliged to supplement the pledged property accordingly.

575. If the obligor is in default with the discharge of a secured claim, the pledgee may claim satisfaction directly from the pledged property without first having to seek in court the discharge of a due claim from the obligor (*realisation phase*).

576. The realisation phase may be implemented in several ways (satisfaction based on agreement between the pledgee and the pledgor or a contracting pledgor, sale in a public auction or judicial sale of the pledged property).

577. The pledgee will notify the pledgor of commencement of realisation of the pledge; the notice must also state how the pledgee will be satisfied from the pledged property, and the pledgee will have the commencement registered in the Land Register. A pledgor must suffer the exercise of a pledge, surrender to the pledgee the pledged property, including the instruments necessary for its takeover, sale and use, and provide him with other necessary cooperation. The pledge as well as pledges with worse positions regardless of the satisfaction of their creditors are extinguished upon realisation of the pledged property.

578. The proceeds of the realisation of the pledged property will be used to cover the principal of the secured claim, the accessories of the claim and the necessary costs incurred in the realisation of the pledge. A secured claim is extinguished only to the extent it was covered from the proceeds of the sale of the pledged property; if a part of the secured claim remains outstanding, the obligee may seek its payment from the obligor. The pledgee is obliged to pay any excess of the secured debt to the pledgor. Where the obligor and pledgor are different persons, the pledgor enters into the rights of the pledgee by payment of the pledgee's claim, and the obligor is obliged to settle what has been provided for him (recourse claim).

579. If bankruptcy is declared with respect to the property that contains the pledged property, that is, *insolvency proceedings* take place, the possibility of realisation of the pledge by the pledgee is blocked (automatic stay)[307] and the creditor assumes the position of a secured creditor. The administration and realisation of the pledged property is taken over by the receiver or a person stipulated in the reorganisation plan; however, the creditor may give instructions to such persons (in terms of administration and methods security). The realisation itself takes place during the insolvency proceedings and the proceeds are rendered to the secured creditors (after deducting the costs of administration and sale).

---

307. Cf. Tomáš Richter, *Insolvenční právo*. (Prague: Wolters Kluwer, 2nd edition, 2017), 263 et seq.

580. If several creditors are secured on the same real property, the rules for the *order of pledges* apply. The basic rule for the assessment of the order is the time of pledge creation. In the case of a mortgage, the moment of delivery of an application to enter a record in the Land Register to the Land Register Office is decisive for the order. Pledgees may stipulate a different order by an agreement in writing. Should any pledges be in the same order, they will be satisfied proportionally.

V. Limitation of Actions and Extinction of a Pledge

581. *Limitation of actions* of a pledge is the consequence of a lapse of the time limit for exercise of a right in court. The limitation period is ten years, and a pledge may not be time-barred before a secured claim is.

582. A *pledge* may be *extinguished* in several ways. If a secured claim is extinguished, so is the pledge. A secured claim may be extinguished especially by discharge, set-off or expiry of time; a secured claim may also be extinguished by discharge by the pledgor. On the contrary, limitation of actions of a secured claim does not result in the extinction of the pledge. A pledge may also be extinguished in the case of concurrent duration of a secured pledge, i.e., upon extinction of the pledged property, waiver of the pledge by the pledgee, payment of the price of the pledged property by the contracting pledgor or the pledgor into the hands of the pledgee, expiry of time for which the pledge was established, acquisition of the pledged property in good faith that the property is not encumbered with a pledge, transfer of the pledged property if the pledge contract stipulates a possibility of its sale without encumbrance, agreement of the parties, withdrawal from the contract or extinction as a result of realisation of the pledge (sale of the pledged property).

VI. Subpledge

583. Subpledge is a special case of pledge consisting in pledging a claim (primary pledge), which itself has a pledge with respect to a secondary pledge (subpledge). In other words, a claim secured by a pledge becomes pledged property itself. The economic essence of a subpledge is that if a secured claim is not discharged by the obligor, the subpledgee may seek its discharge from the primary pledged property (claim of the subpledgee) or directly from the subpledged property, which secures discharge of the primary pledged property. A subpledgee may seek satisfaction from the subpledge as soon as his claim secured by the subpledge becomes due. Provisions on pledge apply to subpledge with the necessary modifications.

Chapter 2. Securities in Movable Property

§1. Privileges

584. Since the CC regulates the basic instruments of security for all property in general, movable property is subject to what has been said in Chapter 2, §1. It should be added here, as stated in Part II, that any property that is not real property is considered movable property, whether tangible or intangible (with exceptions). Due to different characteristics and also due to the existence of older regulation, different movable property have some variations under different regulations but this does not change the essence of security.

§2. Pledge

I. Deviations from Mortgage

585. As already mentioned, a pledge is regulated in general for all kinds of property; what was described in Part V, Chapter 1, §2, therefore, applies to general issues associated with movable property. Legal regulation of movable property, however, shows some deviations, including those that depend on the kind of movable property.

586. The basic difference can be found in the regulation of creation of a pledge. A pledge of movable property is created upon surrender of such property to the pledgee. Surrendering movable property may be substituted by designating the property as pledged (e.g., by a label). If agreed so between the parties, a pledge in real property is created upon registration in the pledge registry, administered by the Notarial Chamber of the Czech Republic. A pledge of an enterprise and of collective property (e.g., an art collection or a herd of cows) is created upon registration in the pledge registry. Registration in the pledge registry is done by a notary who at the same time drafted the pledge contract.

587. In addition to the aforementioned model of creation, there are also other cases of creation of a pledge. A pledge of an aircraft arises upon registration in an aviation registry, of a vehicle upon entry in the vehicle's registration document, of a trademark upon registration in the trademark registry administered by the Industrial Property Office, etc.

II. Pledging a Share in a Corporation

588. It is very common especially in the world of business corporations that an interest (share) in a corporation or its enterprise is pledged. Enterprise is an organised set of assets and liabilities created by an entrepreneur (collective property;

universitas rerum[308]) which is as a whole used to pursue business activities, and a pledge of it is created upon registration in a pledge registry; it is usually understood as a *floating charge* (new components of enterprise become part of the pledge, and components that leave are, on the contrary, released from the pledge). A share in a corporation reflects the rights and obligations of a shareholder constituting his participation in the corporation (where the share is represented by a security, the security is pledged). A corporation is a legal entity in which its shareholders have their shares (company, association, cooperative, etc.).

589. A share in a corporation may be pledged under the same conditions under which it is transferable, unless the founding legal act (articles of association, contract of partnership, etc.) determines otherwise. A pledge is established contractually but is created upon registration in a public register in which the corporation is registered (register of companies, register of associations). In other words, the existence of a pledge of a share in a corporation can be found directly in the register of entities, not in a register of property. Moreover, a prohibition of encumbrance or alienation of a share in a business corporation is also constitutively registered in the register of companies as a right in rem.[309] A secured creditor does not become a shareholder upon the creation of a pledge but it can be, however, stipulated that he may exercise a voting right. Unless it has been stipulated that the pledgee acquires the pledged share at the moment of unsuccessful sale, the pledgee may exercise all the rights of a shareholder until that moment.

590. If a secured claim becomes due, the pledgee becomes entitled to pecuniary and other in rem performances resulting from the interest in the corporation up to the amount of the secured debt (typically a share in the profits, distributed own resources, returned additional contribution,[310] etc.). In the case of realisation of a pledge, the, pledgee notifies all shareholders that the exercise of the pledge has begun. If these shareholders have a pre-emptive right in the share (e.g., in a limited-liability company), they may exercise it during the sale of the pledged property. It may be stipulated that the creditor acquires the pledged share upon an unsuccessful attempt at sale, otherwise he may claim, within one month, that the pledgor transfer the pledged share to the creditor under usual trading conditions in order to discharge the debt (in the event of failure to act, the court may decide on the contract).

308. Cf. e.g., Bohumil Havel, *Závod (podnik), věc hromadná a NOZ* (Prague: Wolters Kluwer, Rekodifikace & praxe, Vol. 12/2012).

309. Jan Dědič in Jan Dědič, Bohumil Havel & Ivana Štenglová, *Zákon o veřejných rejstřících právnických a fyzických osob. Komentář* (Prague: C. H. Beck, 1st edition, 2015), 89 et seq.

310. Bohumil Havel in Ivana Štenglová & Bohumil Havel et al., *Zákon o obchodních korporacích. Komentář*. 2nd edition, (Prague: C. H. Beck, 2nd edition, 2017), 347 et seq.

III. Pledge of Securities or Book-Entry Securities

591. A *security* under Czech law is an instrument (medium[311]) with which a right is associated in a way that the right may not be exercised or transferred without that instrument (e.g., share, bill, bond or warehouse receipt). If a security is not issued in a documentary form, it may be replaced by an entry in a register (administered especially by a central depository), which also reflects all changes in that security – *book-entry security*. Book-entry securities are maintained on property account.

592. In principle, a pledge of a security is created upon delivery of the security to the pledgee; it is also possible to stipulate creation upon registration in the pledge registry. The creation of a pledge of securities to order also requires a pledge endorsement. A pledge of a book-entry security is created upon registration on the owner's account in the respective registry (it is necessary to distinguish cases where the subject of pledge is a book-entry security or an account of book-entry securities).

593. For the duration of a pledge of securities, a pledgee may exercise the rights attached to the pledged securities to the extent stipulated by the parties; however, he does not become a shareholder. The yields and other payments gained from the securities are governed by the provisions on a performance from a pledged claim.

IV. Pledging the Account of an Owner of Book-Entry Securities

594. A pledge of the account of book-entry securities is created upon its registration in this account in the relevant register. Unlike in the case of pledge of a book-entry security, which is always linked to a particular security, a pledge of the account of an owner of book-entry securities applies to all securities registered in the account or accrued during the existence of the pledge. Similarly, in the case of *floating charge*, if securities are transferred from a pledged account with prior consent of the pledgee, the pledge of such securities is also extinguished.

V. Pledge of a Claim

595. In addition to mortgages and pledge of securities, one of the most common pledges is a claim. That means a creditor's right to performance by a debtor, and it concerns movable property which may be pledged under the same conditions as it may be transferred. A pledge of a claim is created when the pledge contract becomes effective, unless a later date is stipulated. It is also possible to stipulate that the creation is conditioned upon registration in the pledge registry.

---

311. Cf. Jindřich Vítek in Petr Lavický et al., *Občanský zákoník I. Komentář. Obecná část (§ 1–654).* (Prague: C. H. Beck, 1st edition, 2014), 1816 et seq.

596. Before a secured debt becomes due, a debtor may only provide performance with respect to a pledged claim jointly to the pledgee and pledgor (or to a depositor, who will surrender the performance to the creditor after the debt becomes due). If a secured debt has become due, the pledgee has the right to have the debtor under the pledged claim provide a performance only to him. Where performance is provided under a pledged claim, the pledgee will surrender to the pledgor everything that exceeds the secured claim, including accessories and the reimbursement of costs to which the pledgee is entitled. If a pledge of a claim from account has been stipulated, the pledgee has the right to order the person who keeps the account to pay him the balance on the account up to the amount of the secured debt, provided that he informs him of the amount and the due date of the secured debt.

597. Similarly, in the case of a global assignment (*see* below in §4, III, A), it is also possible to stipulate a *global pledge of a set of claims*, whether present or future, if such a set of claims is sufficiently determined, in particular with respect to claims of a certain kind created at a particular time, or various claims arising from the same legal cause (this pledge operates similarly to *floating charge*). Similarly, it is possible to stipulate a pledge of a set of claims in a different manner, for example, by stating that the current list of pledged claims changes every month by an addendum to the pledge contract.

598. Similarly to pledge, transfer of a right of ownership in movable property as security is subject to what was set out above in Chapter 1, §3; however, the creation of that right is usually associated with the contract becoming effective. Where a right of ownership is subject to registration in the respective registry, any transfer of the right of ownership as security will also be registered in it (aviation registry, trademark registry, etc.).

§3. Retention Right

I. Nature, Function and Principles of Retention Right

599. Retention right is a security legal instrument that provides the creditor with a material guarantee of discharge of a (usually) due debt by allowing the creditor to satisfy from the retained property if the debt is not discharged even subsequently. Retention right is a creditor's right in rem in property of another. Retention right, similarly to a pledge, has *security* and *compensatory functions*. Retention right differs from pledge especially in the fact that it is created by a unilateral legal act of the creditor. Moreover, only movable property may be retained and, with exceptions, a retention right may be established only to secure an already due debt. A creditor who has a retention right is entitled to a priority satisfaction from the proceeds of the sale of the retained property, even before the pledgee. A pledge and a retention right may co-exist.[312] Given the serious effects of a retention right on the

312. Cf. Jan Petrov in Petrov, Výtisk, Beran, *Občanský zákoník*, commentary on s. 1395.

rights of the owner of the retained property, it is required that the creditor be in good faith that the debtor may entrust the property to him.

600. Retention right is governed by two basic principles. *Accessory nature* – retention right may fulfil its purpose only if the secured claim continues to exist, and *subsidiarity* – retention right may be exercised only if the claim it secures has not been satisfied.

601. The CC regulates retention right in general in Book Three Title Two Chapter Five (sections 1395 through 1399). Sub-cases are regulated in the context of specific contractual types (e.g., retention right of a party to a contract of sale that keeps movable property for the other party to secure a claim consisting in the costs associated with the keeping of the property, or retention right of a lessor in movable property a lessee has on or in the leased property in order to secure a claim against the lessee). The CC also regulates cases of statutory retention right (retention right of an administrator of property of another to secure his claims arising from the administration, retention right of an heir in the bequeathed property, etc.).

II. Elements of Retention Right

602. The beneficiary from retention right is the *creditor* who has movable property of another in his possession. The aforementioned in rem relationship between the creditor who has secured his claim using a retention right and third parties who must not disturb him in the exercise of the right of ownership has to be distinguished from another legal relationship based on which the property became within the control of the creditor. This can be an obligational relationship (e.g., lease, a work) or another in rem relationship (e.g., manual pledge).

603. A retention right may secure a primarily *due debt*. The debt must be due not later than at the time the creditor retained the property. It is not decisive whether the debt is pecuniary or non-pecuniary. A debt which is not yet due may be secured by a retention right if (a) the debtor failed to secure it otherwise although he was obliged to do so under a contract or law; (b) the debtor has declared that he will not discharge the debt; (c) it has become evident that the debtor will fail to discharge the debt as a result of a circumstance which occurred in relation to the debtor, and of which the creditor was not and could not have been aware at the time the debt was incurred.

604. The subject of the retention right may be only *movable property of another*, i.e., belonging to another person than the creditor. A claim may not be retained[313] because a claim cannot be 'surrendered' to the debtor (or anyone else).

313. Performance other than movable property was also rules out by the then literature – Robert Mayr, *Soustava občanského práva. Kniha prvá: nauky obecné* (Brno: Barvič & Novotný, 1922), 226–227 or František Rouček, in František Rouček & Jaromír Sedláček et al., *Komentář k čsl. obecnému zákoníku občanskému. Volume II.* (Praha, 1935), 806.

As regards *intangible property*, book-entry securities may be subject to retention because in this case the content of the right is associated with a determinable medium, which makes them similar to the nature of movable property. Movable property that is subject to retention may be tradable, i.e., transferable to another person.

III. Existence of Retention Right

605. Retention right is created by a *legal act* whereby the creditor expresses his intention to retain the property. It is a *non-addressed* legal act; the creditor is obliged to notify the debtor of the retention. Retention right may not be created in property removed from a debtor by force or trickery or in cases where both parties rule out the creation of the retention right.

IV. Content and Exercise of a Retention Right

606. The content of retention right is the creditor's authorisation to retain property until the satisfaction of his claim or until the extinction of the retention right for another reason. The creditor is obliged to administer the retained thing with due managerial care and is entitled to be reimbursed for the costs by the debtor as a lawful possessor. The creditor may use retained property only with the consent of the debtor and in a manner which is harmless for the debtor. Where the debtor fails to discharge his debt even subsequently, he may agree with the creditor on the manner of satisfaction of the retention right (keeping the property, sale). The debtor is obliged to reimburse the creditor with the necessary costs incurred in connection with the sale of the retained property.

607. Retention right, as a property right, is subject to limitation of actions. However, a retention right does not become time-barred while the creditor has the retained property in his possession or while a third party takes hold of it for the creditor. As soon as the retained property is no longer controlled by the creditor, the retention right is extinguished and, therefore, there is no sense in considering its limitation of actions.

V. Extinction of Retention Right

608. The methods of extinction of retention right – similarly to the case of extinction of a pledge – may be distinguished based on whether the secured debt is also extinguished with the retention right or whether the secured debt continues to exist despite the extinction of the retention right. A retention right may be extinguished as a result of any method of extinction of a secured claim. The cases where a retention right is extinguished although the secured debts continues to exist include (a) extinction of the retained property, (b) waiver of the retention right, (c) loss of the creditor's control over the retained property, and (d) provision of an additional security to the creditor.

609. In insolvency proceedings with respect to the debtor's assets, a creditor with a claim secured by a retention right is a secured creditor and will be satisfied in the insolvency proceedings.

§4. Delegation, Direct Claim (Possibility Created by Statute Law to Claim Payment Directly from the Debtor of One's Debtor)

I. General Subrogation

610. Czech law also regulates consequences of situations where a performance was provided by another person and situations where the positions of parties change during the existence of an obligation – these instruments, however, do not take the form of in rem security. As a result of the aforementioned, the positions of the debtor or the creditor often change, and so does the right of ownership in a claim or debt, either in whole or in part.

611. First of all, a general rule applies that an obligation is linked with contracting parties that created that obligation; however, the creditor usually has to accept performance provided to him (with the debtor's consent) by a third party. The law also provides for *facultative subrogation*, i.e., a rule that a person who performs a debt of another without being liable as a surety or providing any other security for such a debt may, before or upon the discharge of the debt, require that the creditor assigns his claim to him. If a performance is provided for another person for a legal cause, debtor's consent is not necessary, and the person providing the performance enters the creditor's rights *ex lege* upon discharge of the debt and has the right to reimbursement for the performance by the debtor – the creditor's claim passes to such person including accessories, security and other rights associated with the claim (*statutory subrogation*).

II. Voucher

612. A debt can also be discharged by delegation of performance. One possible manner of such delegation is a voucher, which entitles a voucher payee to collect, in his own name, a performance from a voucher payer (debtor), and the voucher obliges the voucher payer to perform to the voucher payee on the account of the voucher issuer. A voucher payer who has accepted a voucher may only assert those defences against the voucher payee which concern the validity of acceptance, invalidity of the voucher or its defects, or defences which are based on an express provision of the voucher or those which the voucher payer is entitled to assert against the voucher payee personally.

613. If a voucher relates to an existing debt relationship between the original creditor and the voucher payor, the voucher payor is obliged to satisfy the voucher, and his debt is extinguished only when he provides performance to the voucher payee (although the voucher payee is not the original creditor). For legal security of contact, the voucher payer is obliged to perform only against the issuance of an acquitted voucher.

III. Change in the Person of the Creditor

A. Assignment of a Claim

614. In business transactions, in addition to goods, which is usually pledged on the basis of *floating charge*, one of the most common instruments of security is a claim (*see* above §3, F). A right arising from a claim, however, may also be transferred directly, that is, not through security. When a claim is assigned, the right of ownership in the claim changes; and since it is movable property, unless stipulated otherwise, the creditor acquires the right of ownership directly when the transfer contract becomes effective.

615. By a contract, a creditor may, as an assignor, assign the entire claim or part thereof to another person (an assignee) even without the consent of the debtor. By assigning a claim, an assignee will also acquire the accessories and rights associated with the claim, including the security for the claim. It is possible to assign a claim which may be alienated, unless excluded by a stipulation between the debtor and creditor. Violation in this rule is, in the majority's view, subject to voidability. It is not possible to assign a claim which is extinguished upon death or the content of which would change upon a change of the creditor to the detriment of the debtor.

Until an assignor informs the debtor or the assignee proves the assignment of the claim to the debtor, the debtor may be released from his duty by discharging his debt in favour of the assignor or making another settlement with him. An assignment of a claim has no effects against a person who secured a debt with a pledge, suretyship or otherwise until the assignment of the claim is notified to such a person by the assignor or proved to him by the assignee. Even after the assignment, the debtor retains defences against the claim which he had at the time of the assignment. Mutual claims which a debtor had against the assignor may also be invoked by the debtor against the assignee, even where they were not yet due at the time of the assignment; however, he must notify the assignee of his claims without undue delay after becoming aware of the assignment. If a claim has been assigned for consideration, the assignor guarantees, with respect to the assignee, the existence of the claim at the time of the assignment and is liable as a surety for its recoverability up to the amount of the consideration received plus interest.

616. It is also possible to assign a set of claims (*global assignment*), whether present or future, if such a set of claims is sufficiently determined, in particular with respect to claims of a certain kind created at a particular time, or various claims arising from the same legal cause. Similarly, it is possible to stipulate an assignment of a set of claims in a different manner, for example, by stating that the current list of assigned claims changes every month by an addendum to the transfer contract.

B. Assumption of a Debt

617. Persons other than the original debtor may enter a debt relationship. If a person and a debtor stipulate that the person will assume the debtor's debt, the person will enter in the debtor's place as a new debtor, subject to the consent granted by the creditor to the original debtor or the person assuming the debt; consent can also be granted in advance. If a creditor does not approve the assumption of the debt, the creditor does not acquire any direct right with respect to the person assuming the debt; however, the person assuming the debt is obliged with respect to the debtor to ensure that the debtor is not required to provide a performance to the creditor (obligational relationship between the person assuming the debt and the debtor).

618. To provide for cases of passage of a registered pledge or another security encumbering property together with the transfer of a right of ownership in property registered in a public register, the law stipulates a rebuttable presumption that the debt secured by the security has also passed – if the original owner was at the same time a personal debtor. However, a security for a debt provided by a third person continues to exist only if the third person consents to the change in the identity of the debtor.

C. Accession to a Debt

619. If a person assumes, without the debtor's consent, the obligation to discharge the debt on behalf of the debtor, that person becomes a new debtor in parallel to the original debtor, both of them being liable jointly and severally.

Where the debt of the original debtor has been secured by a third person, no claim may be asserted against the third person for the failure of the new debtor to perform the debt without the third person's consent.

D. Takeover of Property

620. A special case of change in the position of the creditor or debtor is takeover of proportional property as a whole. If a person takes over from a transferor all property or a proportionately determined part thereof, he will, jointly and severally with the transferor, become a debtor in respect of the debts which are associated with the property taken over and of which the acquirer was or must have been aware at the conclusion of contract. However, the acquirer is not obliged to perform beyond the value of the property thus taken over.

621. In case such property is taken over by a close person of the transferor (e.g., spouse, children), such a close person will, jointly and severally with the transferor, become a debtor in respect of the debts associated with the property taken over; the liability is not limited to the value of the property thus acquired.

The rules on takeover of property do not apply in transformation of a legal entity or in alienation of an enterprise or its branch.

E. Cumulative Novation

622. An agreement to change the content of an obligation extinguishes the existing obligation and replaces it with a new one (novation). However, at the same time, the original debt may be maintained if the existing obligation stands up in parallel with the new one (cumulative novation).

623. A stipulation whereby the former debtor, whose debt is terminated, is replaced by a new debtor having a debt from a separate legal relationship or having a duty to perform a different subject does not have the effects of assumption of debt and is assessed as a novation.

F. Assignment of a Contract

624. It used to be common in business practice to stipulate joint assignment of claims and assumption of debts as an instrument for the takeover of the entire contract.[314] The CC has simplified the situation and provides general rules for contract assignment, including assignment to order (by endorsement).

625. Unless excluded by the nature of a contract (e.g., performance to be provided in person), either party may, as an assignor, transfer his rights and duties under a contract or part thereof to a third person if the assigned party consents to it and if the contract has not yet been fully executed (consent may also be granted in advance). Assignment of a contract becomes effective against the assigned party upon its consent or upon notification of assignment if the assigned party provided prior consent.

626. The purpose of contract assignment is to liberate the assignor from his duties to the extent of the assignment from the moment the contract assignment becomes effective. The assigned party may prevent those consequences by declaring, with respect to the assignor, that it refuses such liberation (unless it has waived such a right). If the assigned party refuses the consequences of contract assignment, the assigned party may require the assignor to perform in case the assignee fails to fulfil the duties assumed.

314. Cf. Milan Hulmák in Milan Hulmák, Jan Petrov & Petr Lavický et al., *Občanský zákoník V. Závazkové právo. Obecná část (§ 1721–2054).* (Prague: C. H. Beck, 1st edition, 2014), 792 et seq.

627. The assigned party also retains all the contractual defences against the assignee. The assigned party retains other defences which it had against the assignor if such retention is reserved in the contract or in the consent to the assignment of the contract.

Selected Bibliography

Alexandra Braun, Anne Röthel, *Passing Wealth on Death: Will-Substitutes in Comparative Perspective* (Oxford and Portland, Oregon: Hart Publishing, 2016).

Astrid Deixler-Hübner, Martin Schauer, *Erbrecht* NEU (Wien: Lexis Nexis, 2015).

Bohumil Havel, *Závod (podnik), věc hromadná a NOZ* (Rekodifikace & praxe, Vol. 12/2012).

Bohuslav Petr, *Nabývání vlastnictví originárním způsobem* (Praha: C. H. Beck, 2011).

Jan Dědič, Bohumil Havel, Ivana Štenglová, *Zákon o veřejných rejstřících právnických a fyzických osob. Komentář* (Prague: C. H. Beck, 1st edition, 2015).

Emanuel Tilsch, *Občanské právo. Část všeobecná* (Prague: Wolters Kluwer, 1925, reprint 2012).

Eva Kabelková, Hana Dejlová, *Nájem a pacht v novém občanském zákoníku. Komentář* (Praha: C. H. Beck, 2013).

Filip Melzer, Petr Tégl, et al., *Občanský zákoník. Velký komentář. Volume 1* (Prague: Leges, 2013).

Filip Melzer, Petr Tégl et al., *Občanský zákoník. Volume 3.* (Praha: Leges, 2013).

Francesco Schurr, *Handbuch des Vermögensschutzes* (Wien: Manz, 2015).

František Rouček, Jaromír Sedláček et al., *Komentář k čsl. obecnému zákoníku občanskému. Volume II* (Praha, 1935).

Gary Watt, *Trusts and Equity* (London: Oxford University Press, 3rd edition, 2008).

Milan Hulmák et al., *Občanský zákoník VI. Závazkové právo. Komentář* (Praha: C. H. Beck, 2014).

Ivana Štenglová, Bohumil Havel et al., *Zákon o obchodních korporacích. Komentář* (Prague: C. H. Beck, 2nd edition, 2017).

Jan Petrov, Michal Výtisk, Vladimír Beran, *Občanský zákoník. Komentář* (Prague: C. H. Beck, 2019).

Jan Sedláček, *Vlastnické právo* (Prague: Nákladem právnického knihkupectví a nakladatelství V. Linhart, 1935, reprint Wolters Kluwer 2012).

Jana Bílková, *Bezdůvodné obohacení v novém občanském zákoníku* (Prague: C. H. Beck, 2015).

Jiří Krčmář, *Práva věcná* (Prague: 1946, reprint 2014).

Jiří Spáčil et al., *Občanský zákoník III. Věcná práva. Komentář* (Prague: C. H. Beck, 2013).

Jiří Spáčil, *Ochrana vlastnictví a držby v občanském zákoníku* (Prague: C. H. Beck, 2005).

Jiří Spáčil, *Věcná břemena* (Prague: C. H. Beck, 2006).

Jiří Spáčil et al., *Věcná práva. Katastr nemovitostí. Správa cizího majetku* (Prague: C. H. Beck, 2018).

Jiří Švestka, Jan Dvořák, Josef Fiala, *Občanský zákoník. Komentář. V. díl* (Prague: Wolters Kluwer, 2014).

Jiří Švestka, Jiří Spáčil, Marta Škárová, Milan Hulmák, *Občanský zákoník. Komentář* (Prague: C. H. Beck, 2009).

Karel Eliáš et al., *Občanský zákoník: velký akademický komentář* (Prague: Linde, 2008).

Karel Klíma, *Constitutional Law of the Czech Republic* (Plzeň: Aleš Čeněk, 2008).

Katerina Ronovská, Petr Lavický, *New Czech Foundation and Trust (Like) Law: Initial Experience and Reactions* (Trust and Trustees Vol 6/2016).

Klaus Müller, *Sachenrecht* (Köln, Berlin, Bonn, München: Carl Heymanns, 1997).

Luboš Tichý, Kateřina Ronovská, Miloš Kocí, *Trust a srovnatelné instituty v Evropě* (Praha: CPK, 2014).

Luboš Tichý, Petra Joanna Pipková, Jan Balarin, *Kupní smlouva v novém občanském zákoníku.* Komentář (Prague: C. H. Beck, 2014).

Madeleine Cantin Cumyn, *L'administration du bien d'autri. Traité de droit civil* (Montréal: Lés Editions Yvon Blais Inc., 2000).

Marek Novotný, Tomáš Horák, Josef Holejšovský, Jaroslav Oehm, *Bytové spoluvlastnictví a bytová družstva. Komentář* (Praha: C. H. Beck, 2016).

Michael Gruber, Susanne Kalss, Katharina Müller, Martin Schauer, *Erbrecht und Vermögensnachfolge* (Springer: Wien, 2010).

Milan Damohorský, *Právo životního prostředí. 3th edition* (Praha: C. H. Beck, 2010).

Milan Hulmák et al., *Občanský zákoník V. Závazkové právo. Obecná část (§ 1721–2054).* (Prague: C. H. Beck, 1st edition, 2014).

Petr Lavický, Jan Hurdík et al., *Private Law Reform* (Brno: Masarykova univerzita, 2014).

Petr Lavický et al., *Občanský zákoník I. Komentář. Obecná část (§ 1–654).* (Prague: C. H. Beck, 1st edition, 2014).

Petr Zima, *Právo stavby* (Prague: C. H. Beck, 2015).

Petr Tégl, *Ještě k některým aspektům zajišťovacího převodu práva* (Obchodněprávní revue Vol. 8/2011).

Radan Marek, Václav Ježek, *Cenné papíry v novém občanském zákoníku. Komentář* (Prague: C. H. Beck, 2013).

Rainer Becker, *Die fiducie von Québec und der trust* (Tübingen: Mohr Siebeck, 2007).

Richard Hemholz, Reinhard Zimmermann, *Itinera Fiduciae: Trust and Treuhand in Historical Perspective* (Duncker and Humbolt, Berlin, 1998).

Robert Mayr, *Soustava občanského práva. Kniha prvá: nauky obecné* (Brno: Barvič & Novotný, 1922).

Roy Goode, Ewan McKendrick, *Goode on Commercial Law* (London: Penguin Group, 4th edition, 2010).

Vladimír Syruček, Vencislav Sabotinov, *Realitní právo* (Prague: C. H. Beck, 2020).

Tomáš Richter, *Insolvenční právo* (Prague: Wolters Kluwer, 2nd edition, 2017).

Vlastimil Pihera, *Nejpodivnější zvíře v lese – poznámky ke svěřenskému fondu* (Obchodně právní revue, Vol. 10/2012).

Vlastimil Pihera, *Krocení trustů Svěřenské fondy v hledáčku první novely občanského zákoníku* (Obchodněprávní revue, No. 5/2016).
Vlastimil Pihera, Kateřina Ronovská, *Fundační principy a hranice jejich flexibility. K otázce možnosti dodatečných změn podmínek fungování svěřenských fondů a fundací* (Právník, Vol. 9/2018).
Wilhelm Felgentraeger, *Friedrich Carl v. Savignys Einfluß auf die Übereignungslehre* (Leipzig: Deichertsche Verlagsbuchhandlung Dr Werner Scholl, 1927).

Selected Bibliography

Index

The numbers here refer to paragraph numbers.

Index

www.ingramcontent.com/pod-product-compliance
Lightning Source LLC
Chambersburg PA
CBHW071447230926
51846CB00001B/370
9789403527338